RETURN TO ZEROPOINT II

Ho'oponopono for a better reality

ROBERT F. RAY

Copyright © 2012 by Robert F. Ray.

All rights reserved. No part of this book may be used or reproduced by any means, graphic, electronic, or mechanical, including photocopying, recording, taping or by any information storage retrieval system without the written permission of the publisher except in the case of brief quotations embodied in critical articles and reviews.

ISBN: 978-1-4525-5559-1 (sc)
ISBN: 978-1-4525-5560-7 (e)
ISBN: 978-1-4525-5561-4 (hc)

Library of Congress Control Number: 2012912782

Balboa Press books may be ordered through booksellers or by contacting:

Balboa Press
A Division of Hay House
1663 Liberty Drive
Bloomington, IN 47403
www.balboapress.com
1-(877) 407-4847

Because of the dynamic nature of the Internet, any web addresses or links contained in this book may have changed since publication and may no longer be valid. The views expressed in this work are solely those of the author and do not necessarily reflect the views of the publisher, and the publisher hereby disclaims any responsibility for them.

The author of this book does not dispense medical advice or prescribe the use of any technique as a form of treatment for physical, emotional, or medical problems without the advice of a physician, either directly or indirectly. The intent of the author is only to offer information of a general nature to help you in your quest for emotional and spiritual well-being. In the event you use any of the information in this book for yourself, which is your constitutional right, the author and the publisher assume no responsibility for your actions.

Any people depicted in stock imagery provided by Thinkstock are models, and such images are being used for illustrative purposes only.
Certain stock imagery © Thinkstock.

Printed in the United States of America

Balboa Press rev. date: 07/17/12

These words will set you free!
I love you
I am sorry
Please forgive me
Thank you

Contents

Chapter 1: Introduction to Return to Zeropoint 1
   Make a New Reality 1
   So, What is Ho'oponopono and Return to Zeropoint? 3
   Mind-Body Connection 7
   The Four Essential Ingredients in Understanding Life 11

Chapter 2: Understanding Return to Zeropoint 12
   Too good to be true? 13
   Disbelief and stubbornness 14
   Brain Effects of Stress Prove It 15

Chapter 3: Preparing to Return to Zeropoint 17
   The Seven Principles 18
   The Three Selves and the Superconscious 18
   Understanding the Three Minds of Humanity 23
   The Setup Statement 25
   Cleaning & Clearing of the Subconscious Mind 26
   I Love You 27
   I Am Sorry 27
   Please Forgive Me 28
   Thank You 28
   Zeropoint and Life Experiences 29
   Return to Zeropoint is both objective and subjective in nature 30
   Understanding the Ego 31
   Control Issues 33
   A little bit about Religion and Philosophy 37

What is Reality? 39
Creating Change Through Meditation 41
Goals..42
Recap 44

Chapter 4: My Own Journey.. 46
Intention vs. Inspiration..47
If I Heal Myself, I Heal My World 49
The World as You Experience It Is Not the Real Deal 50
You Do Not Have to Know How or
Why Data Got There!..51
Exploring the Solutions 52
Who am I? 52
Who is in charge?...53
IF NOT the Intellect, WHO or WHAT is in charge?.....54
Memories Dictate the Experience 54
The World Resides in the Subconscious Mind 55
The Superconscious Mind does NOT
generate ideas, feelings or actions.................................56
The Subconscious Mind does NOT
generate experiences 56
Are My Family and Friends Real? 57
The First Few Times 59
A Closer Look at Zeropoint..60
Common Ground, the EQUALISER of your
True Identity 61
The Ancients Understood This 61
Once the Return to Zeropoint Process Begins,
It Continues 62

Chapter 5: The Advanced Techniques 64
"Seek and you shall find, knock and the door shall be
opened for you"..65
The SOUL can be INSPIRED by Divine Intelligence
WITHOUT knowing what is going on.........................67
Reality and Return to Zeropoint. Will I die? 68

Non-Judgment and Intentionality 72
Why do I let "divine presence" support me? 76
Why do I create these opportunities and experiences? 77
Let me explain my own belief about this emptiness 78

Chapter 6: The Importance of Your Blessing 81
We Constantly Get in the Way of Life 82
Memories 83
Back to business: 88
Personal Loss 91
Relationships 91

Foreword

THERE'S A REFRESHING MOVEMENT awakening in the hearts and minds of humanity, and its transformative potential is inspiring tens of thousands of truth seekers to discover new hope for their future. If you are here now, you are the very person that the world has been waiting for; do not ever doubt this fact.

At the forefront of the movement are a myriad of *lightworkers*. They are people who devote their energies for the betterment of humanity, and getting to know them is one of the biggest joys in life. Now, with the publication of this book, I hope to be added to that group. Join us (myself and other lightworkers) for the *Return to Zeropoint* movement.

By drawing in part from the ancient wisdom of the Huna tradition and developing a remarkably clear, relevant and accessible form of Ho'oponopono that is expanded and far reaching, I am setting a new path for those who want something more for themselves, and who understand that it takes an integrated and multi-faceted approach to heal and eliminate old programming— past hurts and fears— to unleash the untapped potential of the awakened consciousness that exists within each of us.

Preface

Are we witnessing what has been foretold to be the great Ascension? The ending of the Mayan calendar, long touted to be a huge time of change for humanity, has occurred as of October 28, 2011. Hollywood did not write the story correctly. Its version focused on doom and gloom. It is not about gloom and doom at all, but in fact, is the promise of a better future. I am not totally sold on this idea of Ascension, but I do try to do all I can to be as spiritually tuned up and tuned in as I can in all ways, as I enjoy the interaction that I have come to realize and love. The spirit world now is always working within me, and it is such a fabulous way to navigate life.

Hollywood's version of the end of the Mayan calendar is entertainment at best, but it is not reality and was not intended to be anything more than just a movie. Our belief and our reality are different. Ours is playing out for us every day and is doing so in glorious ways. **We are the future hope that we have been waiting for.**

We all have painful memories that have occurred in life, and no one gets by without lumps and bumps. Being born is in itself a traumatic event. The transition from womb to worry is automatic at the very end of the birth canal. We begin worrying about being hot or cold, hungry or full, thirsty or some other concept. The crying that spells trauma, worry, and fear actually begins to take root in the baby. The child that has difficulty with shyness, or the ones so terrified to speak in front of the classroom that they would prefer to just take a failing grade is a sad reality, Those moments supplant memories that damage us and continuously play out in our daily lives. No one escapes his or her own personal terror. So many bad things happen to so many kids, and the memories of traumatic beginnings begin to pile up quickly. It is amazing that we can even escape childhood in one piece.

One thing for certain, we all have memories that we need to confront and dispose of. Ho'oponopono and the *Return to Zeropoint* approach are great tools and will usher in a new reality for each of us, as long as we use the system and do the inner work.

During the time of the Vietnam War, scientists in West Virginia and Princeton, NJ, joined forces to determine if we affect our reality in ways greater than we believed. Special equipment had to be developed so that a truly randomized study could be completed without anyone having any ability to predict an outcome.

Given that nuclear matter—in this case Strontium 90—decays at a rate no one can ever predict, it was chosen as the test material. A minuscule amount of it was placed into a test tube with a Geiger counter and other very sensitive equipment attached. As the electrons were emitted from the sample, it was again proven that the rate of decay was unpredictable and unstable. As the electrons were spinning away from the sample, they triggered a sequence of four switches, which in turn would potentially light a particular corresponding colored light bulb. The rate of cycling was in excess of 1000 times per second. You might agree that while there was or was not a constant fluctuation in the rate of decay, it was far too fast a mechanism for anyone to be able to predict. The mind cannot keep up with the demands of rhythmic movement at that rate of speed, especially when the rate is constantly fluctuating with unpredictable rhythmic results. The machine would stop each half minute or so, and whatever switch was triggered at that fraction of a moment would be reflected in 1 of 4 different colored light bulbs lighting up. Now, viewing the law of averages, since there were only four choices, a test subject could potentially be correct at least 25% of the time.

Results: Average people were right only about 25% of the time, but those with trained minds or empathic power were able to effectively control which switch would trip and light their choice of bulb about 50% of the time. Interestingly, some had the exact opposite effect, but what was learned was that gifted people had a direct effect on the rate of electron emission, resulting in lighting the specific light bulb that they wanted to light. In scientific interpretation, this experiment demonstrated that we have a direct affect upon our reality. The scientific conclusion was that human beings have more affect upon reality than ever before believed. It was a new beginning in our understanding of what reality really is or is not; a new paradigm in our day: **We have an influence upon the reality that we experience, and that influence comes from within our mind.**

Now, influencing reality is nothing new. When I put my key in my ignition and start my car, I have begun to change many things; the burning of fuel, the creation of gases, the spinning of a fly wheel, the movement of wheels, resulting in my ability to drive the vehicle. I know that through my conscious mind, I can initiate actions that change reality from one moment to the next. There is nothing new in that scenario, but that is not what I am discussing here. What about the unexpected? Can I change my reality in other ways? Can I affect you without directly speaking to or directing you in any manner? Actually, science has passed this point and proven the concepts we are teaching in tremendous ways. We stand upon solid ground when we espouse these principals. Join us, and you can find a peace that you never believed you could attain. I wish it for you.

Acknowledgements

Paul Trocola
You share yourself in an unselfish manner. I recognize God within you. You have believed in the good within me, even when I doubted it myself. Thank you for your love and guidance. I couldn't be who I am without you. Aloha!

Jack Flechner
Jacko, you are the critical reader, and you gave me confidence and joy in doing this work. Thank you for your input and for your friendship. I recognize God within you. You are important to me, and I am thankful for you. Aloha!

Trish Vidal
Trish, you are a generous friend, a sophisticated analyst, and a wise spiritual woman. I am so honored to have you as a close friend, confidant, and a diligent and efficient editor. Your input has been invaluable, as has your constructive input. I recognize God within you. Aloha!

Lucille DeFalco
Lucille, you are a generous friend, and a well read and studied spiritual woman. I am so honored to have you as a close friend, and an efficient editor. Your input has been invaluable, as has your constructive input. I recognize God within you. Aloha!

THE AUTHOR OF THIS book does not dispense medical advice nor prescribe the use of any technique as a form of treatment for physical or medical problems without the advice of a physician, either directly or indirectly. The intent of the author is only to offer information of general nature to help the reader in their quest for physical and emotional fitness and general good health. In the event the readers use any of the information in this book for themselves, which is their inherent constitutional right, the author and the publisher assume no responsibility for those actions.

Dedication

I DEDICATE THIS BOOK to the lightworkers of the world, who give their love and tireless energy for the sake of a better day and a hope-filled tomorrow. You bring peace and love to us all. I wish you all a blessing, and I send you all my own: I love you; I thank you; I bless you. And so it is.

Who am I?

I am just an average person who has had extraordinary experiences since I began to use the system that I teach you in this book. I am not a guru or a master. I have never studied Buddhism or other old world philosophies beyond the average educational level. I was a traditional faith follower most of my life and I have a degree in theology. Now I am forever the student of what I am trying to share with you in Return to Zeropoint. I may be inspired to write this book, but that in no way qualifies me as the master or guru. If I was either of them, or even a magician, I would change our world for the better without having to impress upon you with how to do it for yourself. I wish I could do just that. It would be so easy if I could. Unfortunately, we have to understand how reality works in the true sense. We must understand our place in shaping the reality that we experience, as without this knowledge we cannot move forward. It is what I see as the quintessential tool for life.

As a person who believes in the presence of Divine Consciousness within all people, I have a disdain for violence and for the intolerance of anyone or any group. I respect others as I hope to be respected in return. Divine Consciousness equally loves all people, both good and bad. I find it peculiar that some churches will not allow the name of a prison inmate to be spoken aloud from the pulpit so that we may pray for them. They state that the reason for this is that it brings potential scandal to the church. I say that this is small minded, pitiful and wrongful. All people deserve mercy and healing, especially the criminal. Since society has judged them, the church has no need to do so. All people deserve mercy, as mercy is our innermost desire. Churches do enough to bring scandal upon their own image and praying for a criminal has nothing to do with it.

I want to be as fair and theologically unobtrusive as I can be for the sake of people of different faiths. We are going to use the word "Divine Consciousness" to represent what each of us conceives of as that" Higher Power". While we each have a personal belief, or so I assume most people do, I greatly respect varied faiths and religions, and even non-theistic beliefs as well. I opt to use the superlative term, Divine Consciousness, over the more common usage of the word God. No harm results from this; no one should ever be offended, and faith traditions are well respected by this manner of usage. Only when quoting known or popular phrases will I revert to the usage of the word God. I do not mean to offend or disregard the sensitivities of anyone. It really does not matter what we believe, as it works as it works, and nothing can render that ineffective. Believe as you wish.

I believe that all religions will undergo a tremendous change within time, and I actually believe that this process has already begun. I think that religions will come to this change of their own accord, but if they fail to, the public will bring about for them, as people are developing different beliefs no matter what churches stress as truths. Divine is real, but the Divine Consciousness is embedded within each of us. The Divine is closer at hand and more interactive, and requires no institution whatsoever to cooperate or integrate and communicate with us. Churches slow the process down with all the rituals, rules, and methods that they create to connect with the Divine Consciousness, and they will generally warn you that you cannot count upon that fact that Divine Consciousness resides within us all. If we are told we need to do this and that in order to please God, then they are forcing us to distance ourselves from that place within us where Divine Consciousness resides. They set up barricades for us because it keeps them in business. Churches are businesses, and do not ever be led to believe that they are not. They do serve some good, but not enough good for me to stay there. I wish them all peace, but they pose no intrigue for me.

Personally, I am done with waiting for the voter to hit the polling booth to change my life circumstances. I am convinced that politicians are always just that: politicians. If I want a better quality of leader, I can participate with that by beginning within myself. Do I want corruption in politics, religion, and other sectors of the world to cease or improve? I have to begin within me. I am tired of people that drain society by manipulating in an unhealthy way, like the rapist, the criminal, the scam artist, and many other unsavory types? It all begins and completes within me; not by me trying to force change on the outside. I have to change inside, so they can follow suit and change outside of me. I am not speaking of leading by example either. I can, and will, have a huge impact on myself and by extension, upon society as I experience it, by working within myself and projecting a better, kinder, more wholesome reality.

One thing you can count upon; I do not foresee that I will ever do anything in my life that is more important than doing this task right now; for me, for you, for society, and for the future of our world. It is so pure, so fantastic, easy and so effective that I can't believe the world wasn't already made aware of it.

In this book, we focus upon the powerful tool that should be used in the process of returning to Zeropoint–a higher state of consciousness–that potentially unleashes strong inner powers, using an integrated technique that is based upon the ancient approach of Ho'oponopono.

CHAPTER 1:
Introduction to Return to Zeropoint

Make a New Reality

ARE YOU TRULY HAPPY with the way your life plays out? If so, you are a rare diamond. If you believe that your life is so perfect, do you have faith that it will always remain that way? I doubt you do. Have you never lost someone that you love? Have you never had an argument that you regretted having? Have you not experienced a person in any capacity that was authoritarian, abusive, inflexible, or just plain difficult to deal with? Did you wish to change the relationship with that person, or want to get away from them, so you could accomplish something important to you? Did you ever have an argument with a spouse or a parent that you regretted? Have you never been harassed, picked on, yelled at, or even cursed at? These are everyday occurrences that people encounter; sadly, it is life in the twenty-first century.

Movements and actions that have power to transform societies are driven by key ideas that spawn affirmative actions. Here, we are going to present you with a key idea that can transform your reality and, likewise, can potentially transform your life and thereby all of society. Whether or not you fully understand the concept of what we attempt to teach here is unimportant at first. Understanding will certainly come with use, time and practice.

Our current society *must be transformed* in order to survive. This is a fact upon which many, or most, will readily agree. This entire world needs to change for the better. Here in America, the far left and the far right have had their shot at transforming society and both have failed miserably. Something has to give in this mess, in which we find ourselves. So why not take the lead and change it for the better all on your own? Create what we call a "reality shift" for you and for the world.

Is such transformation possible? I certainly believe it to be so… but, to bring about this reality and help it take shape peacefully, we have to begin with working on ourselves. Once we have begun, we will see positive results and will want to continue the transformation by continuing to this work on ourselves. Then, we begin to share it with those we love and respect. It will take on a life of its own.

How can I transform society, or help it transform if I fail to begin with myself? That is what this program is all about; reaching that higher consciousness and transforming self by entering into a better place, a higher plane. In doing this I become, for the first time, in greater control of my life and my circumstances. That is exactly what a famous Hawaiian therapist did. It worked for him, worked for his patients, and it still works in his life.

Recently I read about a Hawaiian doctor who cured an entire ward of criminally mentally ill patients by reviewing their charts and working upon himself. He did not use his time to provide traditional psychological analysis or medical treatment for his sick or mentally deranged patients. He did not use the discipline of his trained medical specialty to treat them at all. He departed from his professional discipline and worked entirely within himself to treat their conditions. His story about these patients and their return to sanity, despite his lack of medical interaction, is what made him famous. It was revolutionary, it was effective, and it was groundbreaking. It was almost *too good* to be true, at least for me.

When I see a professional depart from his or her usual discipline to do something radically different from what is considered the norm in their profession, I become highly suspicious. I expect my physician to listen to my heart and lungs with his stethoscope and

I expect a psychological therapist to listen to me as I explain my feelings when undergoing psychotherapy. This doctor did nothing normal, usual, or expected in the treatment of his patients. Despite this unusual fact, his patients got much better than average results. It did not compute for me; it just did not add up.

I began to fact check the story about him and the patients at the Hawaiian Mental Hospital. It all checked out. It was real, he is real, and it all was TRUE. I was amazed and filled with wonder at the same time. But how could it be? I wanted to learn and understand this, but I realized that meant that there would be some work for me to do. I was still not totally convinced but I was eager to read more about it and to try to duplicate his results. Small accounts of Ho'oponopono and how-to stories were available online, but they did not make me or anyone else into a successful full spectrum user of the system. I began anyway, eager to see if I could duplicate his results using myself as a subject. My rule number one, just as in medicine, is: **Do No Harm, especially to myself.**

So, What is Ho'oponopono and *Return to Zeropoint?*

Return to Zeropoint, and its roots in Ho'oponopono, are existentialism. Simply stated, existentialism is a term derived from a school of 19th- and 20th-century philosophers who, despite profound doctrinal differences, shared the belief that philosophical thinking begins within the subject—not merely the thinking subject but the acting, feeling, living individual—and moves outward from there. In other words, we originate reality with a thought process and manifest that into reality.

Ho'oponopono is a connection with your life purpose through the realization of 100% personal responsibility; a process that will transform you through an enhanced connection with your self-awareness and self-acceptance. Because of this transformation, your connection to the source of Divine Consciousness will naturally increase, as you will connect with your authentic self. This self-discovery will result in a connection to inspirational thought. It is the consummate tool to releasing painful experiences back to their source and empowering you to embrace them. Once embraced, these aspects of you will work for you and not against you, and the data of suppression is melted away. It is a tool to aid you in solving the bigger problems in life and creating self-healing and a joyful existence. Do you want a life of synchronicity? I do, and I am willing to bet your answer is yes too.

Carl Jung, the noted psychologist and philosopher, wrote extensively about the building of a false or errant structure within the human mind, which has an ability to "project" outward and create an "errant" reality. He termed it as the *Shadow Aspect of the Unconscious Mind*. He stated that as individual attention is habitually and excessively focused on the façade of the persona, the deeper, neglected aspects of the personality relentlessly sabotage the individual's intentions (Jung, 1959, p. 123). In order to account for these frustrations, while also avoiding reordering them at their source, the shadow is conveniently projected onto other people and circumstances (Bennett, 1966, p. 119), resulting in what can often be perceived as threatening and unfriendly outcomes (Wilber, 1979, p. 82). Whether the shadow manifests as a political protester who bombs public buildings or as a pro-life religious extremist who assassinates abortionists, it relentlessly represents the qualities that the persona lacks. As such, attentive detection and conscious integration of the shadow would seem to offer a genuine solution to taming the darker aspects of humanity, as well as harnessing its highest potentials, especially if willingly practiced by a growing percentage of the world population.

The Shadow usually points to your secret life, and in *Return to Zeropoint* workshops, this is where we actually begin to shed chaotic data that causes self-judgement and radical projection into our lives. We begin in this place, because it is rarely tapped, rarely embraced and seldom healed, but to do so will transform your reality more than you can envision, until you actually do the work.

Certainly, you have experienced the natural magnetic draw that a baby has upon adults. Friends, family, strangers, everyone is attracted to the mystical personae of a small child. Up to and including around the 7th year of life, a child has a natural "innocence" that is much more than just that. The child enters this world at Zeropoint and it takes time for subconscious clutter to overtake their minds and create what we recognize here as a chaotic reality.

The system that we call *Return to Zeropoint* has the potential to return us to near that same degree of natural magnetism and inner beauty as the child has. This is the goal of *Return to Zeropoint*: to bring us to that state where we can alter our personal reality for the better. When we arrive there, our inherent spiritual nature begins to blossom, our intuitive powers awaken, and our minds are radically transformed. This proves out for us every day with so many people's statements of life transformation. We are literally taking command of our future and directing our world through the gentle cleaning of our own mind. As we progress, the very things we achieve along this path are indescribably beautiful and desirable changes. Your journey of self-realization and inner beauty begins when you start using your mantras, and clean your inner Subconscious Mind clutter. It happens quickly and painlessly.

This is only one aspect of what *Return to Zeropoint* achieves for us. We recognize that *Return to Zeropoint* is a technique that, when used properly and consistently, brings about two prominent effects. It goes far beyond the process of cleaning the learned behaviors and clutter that we have acquired in this lifetime. Dig in, read on, stay with us, and experience a life that you once only dreamed of having.

The first effect of this practice is a significant sense of inner tranquillity paired with, and because of, a reduction of frustration and worry. This is remarkable to experience, and typically happens quickly. If the sole effect of using *Return to Zeropoint* were the sense of calm and relaxation it creates as a result, the practice alone would be well worth the effort. This is only *one* aspect of what it changes.

The second prominent effect of using this system is actually the more remarkable of the two. *Return to Zeropoint* enhances the life experience by replacing our inner clutter and confusion with outward manifestations of improved situations and relationships. We call that process "cleaning" because that is exactly what we are doing. I clean internally and my outward world begins to change for the better.

As I state this, I envision that the companies that make psycho-pharmaceutical drugs are not going to like this at all. I believe that *Return to Zeropoint* can potentially reduce the need for these drugs somewhat and do so rapidly. These results would be irrefutable and unmistakable. Your physician would be among those who notice remarkable changes taking place in you. I am not suggesting you throw away any advice or prescriptions your doctor gives to you. Give this time and opportunity to work for you, and allow your doctor to recognize the effects of improvement of your condition. Allow your physician to direct decisions to adjust, reduce or cease treatment for depression, anxiety, or any medical condition that may afflict you. Trust in the professional system, and allow your doctor to be the one to make those decisions with you for your own safety and health of mind and body.

Can anyone deny that a sense of well being and inner peace is not valuable? It is greatly desirable, of course, and everyone who has felt calm and relaxed (all of us) has enjoyed the feeling of finding inner peace and tranquillity. It is valuable and enriches our life.

Now breathe deeply. The statement I am about to make may be a challenge for some of you. If it is, I can assure you that you will begin to understand where I am coming from as we get into this lesson, and your understanding will further increase with your practice. In terms of your reality, you are the projector; everything else is the screen you project outward. Those things we observe and witness in our experience are our mirror image. We are the SOLE CREATORS of our reality.

Mind-Body Connection

I am going to use a rather strong example so that you can begin to understand our constant battling of some problems, repeatedly. Let us say, for the sake of this example, that person X was mugged and beaten. At the very moment of the assault, the mind stores certain data collected from that experience, such as time of day, place of assault, age of assailant, their race, weight, manner of dress, behavior, smell, etc. At that moment, the brain sends out a rush of short chain peptide linkages that fit into place and enhance these memory receptors. These peptide linkages enhance the memory by connecting with surrounding brain matter, and signalling the brain with an magnified electrical impulse, prompting an infusion of endorphins that will "ease" the pain. This natural "drug" is wanted all the time, and actually becomes a key objective of these receptor sites, so they project and project and project, new situations that utilize these memories, over and over again. It is rather like being on a merry-go-round. We will unconsciously strive to project these memories, which end up creating new circumstances that we must play out and endure, that will give us the same or similar degree of endorphin release. It is like the playing of a tape on an endless loop. The image that comes to my mind is the lab mouse that continuously hunts for his cheese. We are not lab mice. We can make the choice to be healthy. It is time to stop these behavioral tapes and projections into our reality, that cause us additional stress so that we can get our "fix" from endorphins. If we want endorphins, we can exercise or jog, or even swim. Taking the painful projection route is far to stressful and really promotes hardship for us. I for one became weary of those heart-stopping circumstances that always tend to pop up in life.

In addition, each time a heart-stopper occurrence or offshoot appears on the scene, the stress causes a flight or fight response. Adrenaline is secreted, and in response, cortisol is secreted. The adrenaline raises our blood pressure as our heart beats faster, and the cortisol causes many other serious issues like gonadal weight gain, just to mention one offshoot problem. The mind-body connection is serious and has a huge health impact.

In a recent conversation with a long-time and sophisticated Ho'oponopono user, she posed this explanation about the establishing of memory to me. She stated that when a stressful memory is created, it is formed in Right or Wrong, Good or Bad context. In other words, what is good, perfect or correct about the event and its attached feelings and impressions, or what is wrong, viscous, mean or terrible about it? I can see this perspective as valid. She went on to say: At one time, there was a point of creation for that memory and its attached emotional component, followed by a point of destruction, where it became cemented in place by layers upon layers of peptide chains that excite it to produce fight or flight response mechanisms. This rings true to me in a fashion as well. I do not believe that every memory does this, but many problems that stop us dead in place or astound us sure can. She urges that we look at these memories and to consider that something is significant and meaningful about them.

Our goal, through the practice of Ho'oponopono is to transform those layers of peptide chains that excite those memories to produce results. She believes that to clear and clean on those memories can bring us back from the edge of typical Type A behaviors. I find her insights to be interesting, as they are not far from my own thoughts on the process of memory creation. Please understand, this is hypothesis, but it is an interesting explanation, and is probably correct to some degree. I am not a scientist or psychologist, so I can not be too overconfident in my unscientific explanation, but it rings true to me, and I considered it worth mention here.

Ho'oponopono and *Return to Zeropoint* are perfect for an unconscious self-affliction process. We can reprogram these peptide chains and memories, as our minds are re-trainable without long drawn out scenarios of reparative therapies. Therapy, in my belief, focuses on these issues, but depending upon the degree of commitment to the process that the patient has, and the degree of sound and thorough practice the therapist employs, therapy too often falls short of repairing the concepts that prolong self-limiting projections. I am clearly not suggesting that therapy is of no value, but instead pose this theory: psychotherapy is often times an incomplete solution to inner struggle on its own. There is always work that the patient must complete. Therapy can aid us in grasping a focus, a perspective, but we cannot place the sole burden of adjustment upon the professional. We must complete that work by fully participating in our recovery from traumatic situations. Now, paired together, they are an outstanding set of mutually complimentary modalities.

Many people have been abused and/or violated; probably more of society than we would guess or believe. Abuse is violent in nature, and PTSD most often results from the extreme shock of victimization. At the moment the shock takes place, dissociative (escapism) behaviour often sets in to ameliorate the severity of the moment, and it too often becomes a lifelong habitual pattern for the victim. *Return to Zeropoint*, being a multi faceted treatment, can reduce tendency to dissociate and the constant tendency to run away or quit every time that there is an argument or stress builds up too high. Once done, cleaning and clearing on memory-by-memory, a new person will undoubtedly emerge, and a healthy mind and body can be the result.

Providing inner peace and correct mental perspective is one thing, but most of us instantly and completely reject the notion that using some technique or another can literally change life and physical health for the better. It would seem to be like a fairy tale, too good to be true. Well, if you just were to try, and give it a go, you too would experience the transformative process that makes for a sound mind body connection.

Perhaps we can turn that around for you and give you a new perspective on Ho'oponopono and the *Return to Zeropoint* practice. Neither practice is what we would consider magical; it is not about stating desires and they are just granted; that is **not** its function. This practice is not the genie that grants us our wishes. Unfortunately, no one else can possibly clear away the wreckage that keeps us from reaching our greatest potential. We alone are in the driver's seat and this seemingly daunting task is entirely up to us. This practice of Ho'oponopono does make it a manageable task.

Return to Zeropoint is about letting go and allowing the Subconscious Mind to rid itself of the imprint of data until it is cleaned cleared and our mind becomes perfectly free once again. With our system and practice, your ego has little bearing—minimal say in the matter. We choose to adjust and attune ego driven mindset and encourage it with sound knowledge, truth, and thought. It is worth the effort, and it is not so difficult. There is no pain involved for our *Return to Zeropoint* users.

None of what we teach in *Return to Zeropoint* is about instant results. Often times they might come, but this is not a quick fix service. So many programs and therapies that are available are simply band-aids. They do not heal the injury at the core; they only cover it up so it doesn't become infected.

This is a process in which the subconscious mind must realize that cleaning and clearing is of benefit. As it does, corrupt data is released, then replaced by Zeropoint, which freely fills the space that was once crowded in darkness. Effects of *Return to Zeropoint* unfold in perfect time. This may not be in your time, but it will always be at the proper time for you to realize change and benefit from it.

Patience is essential in properly using *Return to Zeropoint*. Your trust or belief in it is not essential. It will work for you, despite any disbelief, as long as you properly implement the steps to the process. There will be plenty of times that you might use it and see immediate results, but I forewarn you that this is not always the case. Therefore, steadfastness and adherence to the process is all that is necessary. You will get the hang of it. It will become a part of your natural actions.

The Four Essential Ingredients in Understanding Life

1. Awareness
2. Forgiveness
3. Acceptance
4. Flow

Awareness: This aspect of life transformation is about taking 100% responsibility for each aspect of our experience, no matter who or what is involved. We are the projector; the world we experience is our screen, rather as if we were staring into a mirror. Everything you experience is a projection from within yourself.

Forgiveness: To radically accept your nature and forgive yourself for your unknowing projections. We do not know, nor can we know at this time, how or why we project the things we do, but we forgive and let go. I forgive myself for each error in thought and projection.

Acceptance: I accept myself and my path as my true journey.

Flow: To enjoy the comfort of allowing life and circumstances to unfold for you.

Chapter 2:
Understanding Return to Zeropoint

IN TERMS OF SPACE and mass, we must look to the wonders of our universe for a clue about what we consist of. As we look outward into our universe, we find a great deal of dark matter surrounding seemingly little bits of planets and stars and some asteroids. Science is actively adopting a new theory that explains our case. Science is experiencing that there is a greater energy within dark matter than there is in the planetary or solid matter that dots it. In fact, there is approximately a trillion times more energy than in the planets, stars, asteroids and space dust. In addition, the scientific world is actually calling the dark matter **Zeropoint Energy**.

Now, pause to think for a moment. Wouldn't it seem probable that where there is energy, there is intelligence and purpose? Even the lightning storm, threatening as it may be, has a grand purpose. That purpose is in perfect order with all life and consistent with reality. Lightning is of vital importance to earth. It cleans and clears the earth we call home and provides some of the necessary energy within soil for plants to grow healthily. Imagine how negatively the circle of life could be impacted if there were no lightning storms.

The same is true with the Zeropoint we hope to reach within our own self. Zeropoint is actually the vast "emptiness" that the Dharma traditions like Buddhism and Hinduism seek to achieve. It is our belief that it is far more organized than the dense matter surrounding it. It is pure, unfiltered, un-influenced intelligence. This energy is the very place where Divine Consciousness is free to act, enrich, and influence all that our purpose is based upon. Our cells, as in the outer form of dark matter in deep space, have 90% empty space. That same truth is the space in memory, and it becomes infused with peptides that disrupt its basic purity and simplicity, enhancing our memory impact on brain matter, and therefore our projection of reality.

Can you just feel the love and respect I have come to feel for this methodolgy? I hope I am influencing your thought. I hope to inspire you, as I am greatly inspired.

Too good to be true?

If you stick with it, are consistent in your application, and patient in your outlook, Ho'oponopono and *Return to Zeropoint* will show you extremely worthwhile results. In addition, the results will undoubtedly make your life easier and better. Are you willing to put in the effort and time?

In order to succeed in this practice, become proactive by lovingly encouraging your ego to cooperate and allow you to move forward with ease and confidence. I offer pathways to help you bring your ego into full communion with this new reality, without pain or extraordinary effort. Our system of taming the ego is relatively effortless. Ego is not inflexible, but in fact, it is actually quite reasonable and loving. Ego will eagerly yield to logic and reason. This is ego-friendly work, as no one else need be privy to your inner work with the *Return to Zeropoint* methods; there is no cause to feel shame, nor is there any self-abandonment. We do not lead you into a violation of self-identity. Our system is simple work, and is not offensive or challenging. Once done, you are open to realizing your potential as a co-creator, not a victim of faulty thought, driven by an overworked and over burdened ego. We will share a tool that we find valuable, to help you to bypass egocentric influence that would block your objectivity.

So again, can this work for you? Yes. It sure can work for you. The results are entirely up to you.

Disbelief and stubbornness

When naysayers reject the concept that Ho'oponopono can accomplish anything, we begin to use the system of Ho'oponopono to clean and clear their resistance to truth. We can do that work completely within ourselves, not having to insist in any manner that they realize their resistance and without urging them to clear themselves. ***They are merely a projection of our own inner inflexibility and resistance, part of our own defensive Ego-driven components.*** It is true; they are merely a mirror that reflects our inner data back to us. Now that is a crucial fact to accept, and we realize that it is. Do not abandon this concept though, because just as you may be a disbeliever, realize that I was once too. I struggled through the exact same challenging disbelief and resistance that you might be experiencing. I am certainly glad that I persisted in using the system. You can be too and all that you have to do is remain steadfast and continue to employ the steps we teach. As I stated already, you do not even have to have belief in them for them to work for you. Trust is not an essential ingredient for Ho'oponopono or *Return to Zeropoint*. Simply use it, as it causes no harm to anyone.

I was a childhood rape victim, and I totally blocked that from my memory until I began to "break down" many years later. I had the PTSD, and I was always dissociating, as it was a learned behavior from that very first day. When emotional pain became overbearing, I would run away and refuse to work it out or participate in it. Typical *dissociation* is what that is called. That was then, and now I am so different and so much more functional. My inner anger is gone from my psyche. My tendency to run away every time the pressure builds up is gone too, and now I am whole and I actually love myself because of the healing I have experienced. I do understand that not everyone has such deep and scarring circumstances in life, but be warned, you do NOT necessarily remember all that might have happened to you that has resulted in damaging beliefs and behaviors you may harbor within your subconscious mind and your Ego.

Brain Effects of Stress Prove It

There is another, less thought about situation that calls for a real stress-busting system such as *Return to Zeropoint* to be employed. Science has been hard at work to understand the mechanisms in the human brain that help us deal with stress. We certainly understand that stress busting has led to sales of numerous tranquilizers, anti-depressants and lots and lots of alcohol.

Firstly, let us understand when and how the brain is designed to cope with stress. During the process of coping, our brains release complex chemical secretions that help us manage the increase of stressors. These chemicals play a role in establishing what we call the "*fight or flight syndrome*," a powerful autonomic and instinctual response mechanism that is designed to keep us from harm. It is built in. Each time this is prompted by a response to stress, our body takes a veritable beating from it. It can save our life if it happens at the right time, but it can reduce our good health if it happens needlessly and often.

When the Fight or Flight Syndrome begins, huge surges of adrenalin and noradrenaline are rapidly supplied into the bloodstream to speed the heart rate. The whole process then narrows the arteries. Blood is then moved out of small vessels into the arteries, and begins to increase the pressure there. The blood races wildly to the extremities, to infuse them with oxygen. In less threatening or less dangerous situations, this is not at all healthy. The next this response does is to prompt the pituitary gland to release cortisol. This is another kind of serious problem for us. Cortisol, a natural compound that the body produces to reduce inflammation, is similar in many ways to cortisone. Each time cortisol is released in quantity, it prompts belly fat to build up, the blood also begins to acidify, calcium is then robbed from bones to neutralize the acidity in the bloodstream, and the arteries begin to occlude from the calcium that now binds with fats in the blood. They combine and stick to the artery walls. From all of this we will get our coveted dose of endorphins to ease the strain we created for our body. At times the process can move us into an effective and rapid response, and at other times just rattle us silly, as if we are being chased.

The next coping mechanism is during sleep. Rapid Eye Movement, which occurs about 3-5 times during an average night's sleep, begins to draw images that we call dreams. This is in part to compensate and work out the stresses we hold from the experiences we have had and the thoughts that plague us. Bad dreams or nightmares can cause disturbed sleep patterns, and actually prompt more fight or flight syndrome. We now see how we can actually be harming ourselves by not coping and removing these errant and chaotic memories during our waking hours. These terror-inducing dreams can wake us and rob us of precious sleep that is needed to keep our bodies running.

Now, imagine, as these stress inducing situations come up during our day, if we employed *Return to Zeropoint* wisely, and cleaned upon those situations that stress us, we could have a healthier body and mind, lower blood pressure, better overall health. That should get your attention. Now, there is one more huge reason to begin to use this system constantly.

Awareness is the key. If we can manage to create the cleaning and clearing disciplines of *Return to Zeropoint*, and we condition ourselves to "train" like this on a regular basis, we are destined to win.

CHAPTER 3:
Preparing to Return to Zeropoint

A FOUNDATION OF *RETURN to Zeropoint* is for us to remain within ourselves and not become concerned and/or caught up in what appears to be happening externally within others. What matters most is what is going on within you and your own mind, namely, your subconscious mind. Another person's rejection of Ho'oponopono is generally just a projection of the distrust, the rigidity, and inflexibility within us. We create them in this manner to project components of our own self-protective and naturally ego-driven existence. It deceives us greatly to do this, but it is merely a learned and well practiced human trait. This is what we are: We are merely human. This pattern of rejection and disbelief began to disappear within me as I began to use this system increasingly and devotedly. Take care of that, beat it, surpass it, and win by retraining your Ego; by sending it love. Everything will be fine and will fall into place within you. This is *Return to Zeropoint*: A practice that establishes renewed sense of inner harmony.

Only two emotions are attached to memory:
1. Love
2. Fear

Of the two things that exist, only Love is real. Fear is merely projected and is ego driven. Fear is merely a lack of love. We must send love into our fears to transform them and thereby gain a new sense of serenity onto the reality that we project.

In any situation where an element of painful memory is remedied, it is possible that something else can be put in place so that it does not re-establish the original imprinted memory pattern in if it wasn't fully cleaned for any reason. This rarely happens, but is a sign that full cleaning and clearing did not actually take place, or that perhaps a blockage exists. When we remedy feelings and emotions through the practice of Ho'oponopono, it is possible to reinforce that cleaning with reassurance and love, which is an easy added safeguarding step.

The Seven Principles

The basic principles of our teaching are these:
1. The world is exactly what you project.
2. There are no limits to possibility or to reality.
3. Energy flows where your attention goes. (Consistent with Law of Attraction)
4. Now is the moment of power, as this moment is all we have ever had.
5. To love is to be happy and joyful with something.
6. All power comes only from within.
7. Effectiveness is the measure of truth – nothing else.

The Three Selves and the Superconscious

Human behavior and experience can be explained, and changed, through the interaction of three inner minds and Divine Consciousness.
1. The Divine Consciousness (Kane) is the source of inspiration.
2. The Super-Conscious Self (Aumakua) imagines.
3. The Conscious Self (Uhane) is awareness.

4. The Subconscious (Unihipili) remembers, transmits, and creates.

Superconscious Mind: Often thought of as the soul, this mind is the one that brings information from Divine Consciousness into the other forms of consciousness. It carries inspirations into our conscious mind for impression and understanding, so that we may act upon them

We should note that Universal or Cosmic Consciousness are concepts common to those with metaphysical philosophies. We are NOT defined as metaphysical in our approach, however, as we are a reality-based system dealing with an honest and true reality based method. Metaphysical teachers appreciate us. Our system is also of great value to those who do not subscribe to metaphysical methods and practices. *Return to Zeropoint* and Ho'oponopono happen to resonate with all philosophies and faiths, as it is in harmony with all of them. This is merely because of the fact that it is a truth, and a reliable system of changing reality that is not fantasy, superstition or mysticism. Though it might appear to us to be mystical practice, it seems as such only because it was unknown to us prior to this time.

Conscious Mind: The Conscious Mind is like a mom. As a mother to the Subconscious, it has a limited ability to store data for the short-term. It has a basic purpose, which is to analyze and "process" data. It is strong. It is Ego influenced, and the ego can strive at first to insulate us from what it considers wrongful blame. The *Return to Zeropoint* method looks upon the Conscious Mind as the Mother to the Subconscious, and as such, it will lead the subconscious to clean, so that we reduce the peptide chains that were formed by strong influence of shock, fear, and anger. These peptide chains, seated within the memory sites in our brain, stimulate our surrounding brain matter and send a request for endorphins. Endorphins are the natural narcotics that we crave and get in abundance when we vigorously exercise or jog.

The Conscious Mind must send the message of love and concern, for joy, peace, and a better existence to the Subconscious Mind. This will relax and disarm our Ego response to challenge of philosophy. Then the subconscious will not be conflicted in receiving the *Return to Zeropoint* cleaning Mantra from the Conscious Mind. It is a delicate relationship of trust, and after a lifetime of mishandling, it has been trained into autonomy as a self-protection against any abnormal or strange influence. We are gently retraining our ego and establishing a healthier and loving relationship between the two realms of information storage and processing.

Subconscious Mind: This powerful area of memory is often projecting into our reality for the sake of creating a situation that will prompt the brain to release four major elements; adrenaline, noradrenaline, cortisol and endorphins. Our brain seeks drugs, and it is not concerned that it might just be creating chaos to get them. Data that does not connect with any apparently valid purpose or meaning is rather like a dog chasing its own tail. We typically respond by conscious mind action, and do an enormous injustice to ourselves by operating solely within that Conscious Mind. It is as if conscious mind is all we have to draw upon to counter problems. We consistently fail to recognize the power within our varied forms of consciousness and our ability to be cleaning out the errant subconscious memory that contributes to constructing a problematic reality.

Example: A friend or loved one becomes ill.

If it is in our world, it is of our creation. Why would we intentionally create a sickly person? Put quite simply, we do not do that with an evil or malevolent intent. That is a common errant perception and misunderstanding of how we operate or what Ho'oponopono or *Return to Zeropoint* is. The parent does not "create a child who is ill". It is either a life path or it can be chaotic data, spinning out of control and trying to make sense out of confusion. Either way, we should view the situation as an opportunity to clear and clean.

Note: If in fact an illness is spiritually necessary for us to endure, no amount of cleaning will remove it, but we sure might alleviate some suffering and pain that might be associated with it. So always clean, and realize that there are no failures in *Return to Zeropoint*. Sometimes illness is simply a necessary aspect of life, and life has a course and a direction to it. Inability to bring about total healing is not a failure of Ho'oponopono or *Return to Zeropoint*, but often times it can bring about healing in ways you might not have imagined. This is why I always caution against clearing and cleaning with a predetermined expectation of what the outcome will be. Do not do that to yourself, as it sets you up for disappointment. Clear and clean with trust in proper outcomes. Leave the presumptions behind and accept perfect order.

However, when it takes time for us to manifest a brighter reality, it can be a clear sign to us that we might have missed something important for us to clean out. Blockages can and do exist within our mind. Keep up with the cleaning and do not give up cleaning until all emotion is surrendered and ended. If you suspect that you might have stumbled upon a blockage, have a conversation with your Subconscious Mind, asking it to enlighten your Conscious Mind as to what the real problem might be. You do this if you think that you have missed something. Your subconscious will begin to trust you and cooperate more fully with you. Remember the mother-child relationship and use that analogy in a loving way to coax assistance from your subconscious.

The man who brought this to the forefront in our time used this methodology to clean a ward of mentally ill patients. Many of them were murderers, rapist and violent people, and they were diagnosed as insane. He never met with them, except on *casual* terms, **not** for therapeutic or medical reasons. He only did chart review and Ho'oponopono cleaning, and they healed. All but two had been cured. The ward is now closed, and this came to be fulfilled within 2 years of his being hired.

Remember, outward problems are a reflection of impressions and feelings that are being triggered in an infinitely chaotic manner. We look through our eyes upon a mirror image of what we have inside us. If chaos is present within, it will become manifest in our world.

We do not even begin to understand the extreme power of the human mind. Science amazes me when it states that we only use about ten percent of the human brain. That is only because science, on a whole, has thus far failed to identify the purpose of the other ninety percent of our brainpower.

Always remember to be aware, cautious and careful: Clean your way through life. It is the only way to alleviate unnecessary problems. Begin the practice and see how much easier life becomes for you and those around you that you have cleaned upon. It is amazing, and it is a gift to us. This is how you can create a true blessing and a widespread ripple effect out into the world.

Understanding the *Return to Zeropoint* mode of action is only dependent upon an understanding that we function on several different levels all at one time. In the Hawaiian, and in esoteric traditions, the second, third and fourth levels are referred to as the Three Minds of Humanity. We illustrate them here, not to confuse or mix philosophies, but just for a broader understanding.

Understanding the Three Minds of Humanity

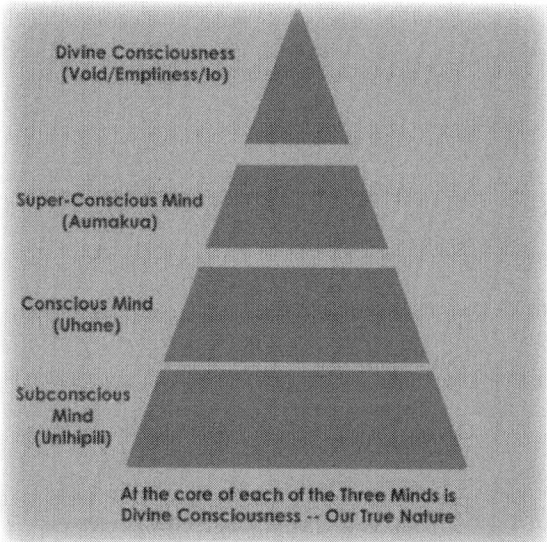

1. The ***Divine Consciousness Mind*** (called the "Void", "Creative Intelligence" in the Buddhist tradition, or as it is known in our world--Zeropoint) is within us and always inspiring us. What is necessary is for us to free up the space necessary to hear the message. Enough cannot be said about this great gift. Every major religion has put their hat into this ring, admitting that the Divine Consciousness is an inextricable part of human experience, intertwined in a mysterious and wonderful way. This is fully affirmed by common faith traditions.

2. There is a "***Superconscious Mind***" (called Aumakua in Hawaiian), which some traditions may refer to as the Holy Spirit. This is where the message from the Divine is translated and disseminated to our lower mentality and understanding via the Conscious Mind and Subconscious Mind. Some people believe that the Super Conscious Mind is one that is. That would be Collective Consciousness as it would be collective in nature.

3. **Conscious Mind** (called Uhane in Hawaiian): where we actively choose; where we compensate; where we adjust concepts and think in real time. This mind has a small capacity and can only process a given amount of information.

In his book *The User Illusion: Cutting Consciousness Down to Size,* science journalist Tor Nørretranders creates a different image of what Consciousness really is and is not. He cites recent research, particularly that of Professor Benjamin Libet of the University of California San Francisco, that shows that decisions are made before Conscious Mind makes them, and that the intellect is only conscious of between 15 or 20 bits of information per second out of a potential.

It is no wonder we spend our lives wandering around looking for answers to life and most often failing to find them. It all comes down to the extremely limited ability of the Conscious Mind. Do not get me wrong; the Conscious Mind is invaluable to us. It has its function and its job to do, and it does it well, but it cannot do everything, nor can it manage to accomplish the job of the Subconscious Mind.

4. **Subconscious Mind** (called Unihipili in Hawaiian): The Subconscious Mind is a very important part of you. This area of the human brain is massive in its storage capacity, and constantly hard at work, 24/7. Think about it for just a moment. Here's a part of you that runs your body; it makes your heart beat, causes the blood and lymphatic systems to circulate, prompts your breathing, causes your eyes to blink, your stomach to digest your food and eliminate waste, and many other tasks that you never even thought of. How aware are you of all the various things that your Subconscious Mind does? Maybe more importantly, how well do you know your Subconscious Mind? Do you consider your Subconscious Mind as a close and trusted friend, or are you at odds with your subconscious? The ancient ones taught that really trusting and getting to know your Subconscious Mind was a very important task—the first step. Whatever your relationship with

your Subconscious Mind, you will probably find that you are much closer to it than ever before as you read on.

Your Subconscious Mind has probably a million times greater capacity to process data than the Conscious Mind has. Where we might think of the Conscious Mind as a smart-phone, you can compare this area of your brain to the supercomputer in its size and capacity. That is a vast difference in capacity to store information.

It is our belief and necessary for a greater understanding of *Return to Zeropoint*, that the Subconscious Mind must be cleaned, allowing clean and clear data to be sent on to the Conscious Mind and into the projection field, for a better experience in life.

The Setup Statement

For the first week of using our system and before I begin cleaning and clearing using *Return to Zeropoint* statements, I use the following statement on myself, as an inner appeal to put things into the proper perspective. In my use and practice, it aids in aligning my ego. The ego is there to protect us, and will vehemently protect us from accepting responsibility for something done by another person. Upon using this tract of words, we begin to relax the over-protective ego and soothe it into cooperation.

> *Great Super Conscious mind, as you are a great source of internal strength, I inform you that I will now begin to use phrases to clean my Subconscious Mind of damaging data and the peptide connections that strengthen painful memory, and set it all into an orderly and clean state. I do this to eliminate the elements that are damaging to my inner peace and well-being. I do this for the benefit of projecting a better reality for me and for others. I will begin to heal myself on many levels, and I ask that you to cooperate, as these corrections will create a peaceful existence and experience for me in my life.*

Ego, I ask that you allow me this opportunity to heal and repair from error in my understanding and beliefs. This is essential for me to accomplish in my life, as these lessons must be learned by me in order for me to move forward and grow in truth. I can adequately control my reality and live out a joyful and rewarding life through this work.

Divine Consciousness, I ask you to guide me in the needed tasks and infuse me with the knowledge that will benefit my life experience for all good reasons. I ask you to increase within me, and help me to mature in wisdom; to complete all necessary tasks for my wholeness and goodness.

To all error standing in the way, I must learn these concepts in order to accomplish wholeness:

I love you.
I am sorry.
Please forgive me.
Thank you.

To all parts of my mind and body, and to all of my nature:

I love you.
I thank you.
I bless you.

And so it is.

Cleaning & Clearing of the Subconscious Mind

To effectively bring this process into your practice on a continual basis when you might want to use it, memorize the following basic

statements. Learn them well, to be said in any manner or any order, in your own native language:
1. I love you.
2. I am sorry.
3. Please forgive me.
4. Thank you.

It is possible to use fancy and foreign words or chants to do this. We are not really in favor of that practice, unless you really understand the language used. We advise you to avoid getting too fancy. These words work; and they work very well, all on their own. Keep it simple.

I Love You

Love has always been a great healing power. Sending all parts of your Consciousness a message of love will resonate through your entire being and generate an immediate feeling of well-being by combating stress.

Once again, being pure spirit, Divine Consciousness is complete and perfect on its own and does not require your love, but the very act of thinking loving thoughts will tune your entire mind to the proper frequency of repair and reordering with demonstrable results.

I Am Sorry

This statement opens the pathway to internal self-atonement. The moment you take responsibility for any negative manifestation you experience or witness you also create an opportunity for the needed internal healing. We have no need to understand how we did any wrong, or why. The apology is not directed to the Divine Consciousness or to anyone but ourselves. Divine Consciousness is purely Spirit and does not need or care about our apologies. Our apology is an inner acknowledgement that we are sorry for whatever it is that we have done to cause the negative and unwanted circumstances to take place, and we are making this statement to our own mind, not someone else.

Just a simple "I am sorry" will suffice. Just keep it simple.

Please Forgive Me

We are asking for forgiveness from our Higher Self for having forgotten the essential need for self-love. We are asking for forgiveness for having shut out so much of the love from our lives and thereby missing out on many wonderful experiences.

We ask for forgiveness with the absolute certainty that forgiveness is granted. At the very core of our being is pure Spirit and Unconditional Love, incapable of feelings of anger, resentment and the other behaviors rooted in neuroses that afflict humans. The Conscious Mind has no bearing here, as Conscious Mind does not participate in the projection of reality, since that reality is projected by our beliefs, impressions and a myriad of chaotic data that is anchored to our memories.

Remember, *Return to Zeropoint* users never have to forgive anyone, since they realize that all wrongdoing is the result of their own wrong action or memories—past or present, and totally born within and projected outward from within us. Whatever your concern, the moment you take responsibility for its occurrence and seek a remedy via *Return to Zeropoint*, you are assured to get a favorable response.

Thank You

Almost invariably, the response might not be what you expect-- but is in fact precisely what you need to begin the process of healing and reconstruction. The gift given in return for these statements will always be perfectly suited for you. Your "thank you" is the acknowledgement that your request for relief of a situation has been heard and acted upon.

The point we always strive to achieve, the point of being totally clean, or as clean as possible, is called Zeropoint.

Zeropoint and Life Experiences

I remember my mom spanking me when I was a child. That was the custom of those years, and it caused me to feel unloved. So with that in mind, I repeatedly state my four phrases as my mantra. I will get to a certain point and my negative memory and emotion disappears and I am done. I still remember my mom spanked me, but no longer feel unloved. I feel nothing, and my inner child is relieved.

I was forced to get in front of my classmates and give a book report. I froze with fear. It made me feel like the world saw me as a stupid kid. I was humiliated. As a result, I still have problems speaking in public. With this in mind, I use my four phrases repeatedly until I feel a diminished emotion and know it is gone. I am done at that point. I will not suffer that any more.

I have a co-worker who constantly irritates me. She always wears clothes that smell like mothballs. I can't stand that. I have that in mind as I begin my mantra and repeat it. I remove my strong emotion to her smell, and the following week, she announces that the allergy she had for years was to mothballs. She stops using them. My mantra served me well.

I walk into a bank. I visit the loan officer to get a car loan. The officer keeps me waiting and is almost annoyed at me which makes me feel insecure about my loan application. I begin clearing with my mantra, remove my concerns, and the officer comes to me an deeply apologizes for having me wait so long. The loan officer actually bends over backwards to make up for my inconvenience. Now that is what I call success.

I have a sibling I have not spoken to in years. We drifted apart. We are so different in philosophies, but we really used to be so close. I miss my brother. I see my hurt, and I clean and clear on that with my mantra. The next day, I had no emotional residue, so I took a leap of faith, picked up the phone and called him. What I got was a warm response with good vibes that were so evident. We both won on that issue.

As I said before, we clean on everything. We clean on the past, the present and the future.

Tomorrow, beginning a new job, I have so many unknowns that I have to face. I do not know who my co-workers will be. I do not know the personality of the individual that will be supervising me. It causes me grief and fear to have these thoughts. I clean on them so that when I walk through the door I get no negative reactions to my presence, and I have a far easier transition through the introductions and training phase of this new position. It goes smooth and easy for me. That saved my day. I began my new job with ease.

Return to Zeropoint is both objective and subjective in nature

Our system is intended to accomplish or attain a result within the mind of the individual, and is the result of the thinking person or subject's efforts to improve the conditions in their subconscious memories.

Return to Zeropoint IS NOT:
- About allowing our ego to lead and dictate an outcome. We will not continue projecting an errant reality.
- Focusing our effort upon a desire, and expecting it to be acquired.
- An effortless practice. It is by no means difficult or exhausting either. It is simple and gentle. It packs a great deal of power. It should always be employed with constancy and consistency.

Return to Zeropoint IS:
- Putting the ego gently and lovingly to rest and in place as much as is possible and trusting in your Higher Self — whatever that means to you.
- A belief that everything you view and witness come from within you and not from any external sources (as we learn in the foundational practice of Ho'oponopono).
- A miniscule amount of effort, and a slight bit of invested time, producing order so you can see dramatic results.

- Much easier than trying to force outcomes to be produced by the external world.
- Extraordinary... and even amazing, if you give it a decent chance.

Understanding the Ego

Ego has a bad reputation. Whether or not we like to admit it, it does have a purpose. Ego is similar to the inflated rubber tire that wraps around the rim of the wheel on which it is mounted. In this instance, the rim is representative of life, and that rubber tire (Ego) shields the rim from the lumps and the bumps of the road. It is simply an effective and efficient defense mechanism: a shield: a protector. Ego should always recognize real danger and help motivate us to avoid it. If Ego causes us to argue with someone we love, it is probably just overworked and overburdened.

Nearly all of us are over-shielded by a subconscious driven ego. The main reason is that we are hooked on always being in control, through errant ego driven motives. Learn to move ego gently to the side, let it off the hook and allow it to relax. It learns quickly too. Even psychologists would tell you that it is worthy to correct and reshape our ego. An ego that is out of control is a sure sign that we are struggling to control things way too much. It is a slippery slope, and often ends in disastrous outcomes.

Where ego becomes troublesome is when this defender tends to overtake all that we are and all that we do. It too often trains us to operate and remain in a fear-minded zone. This is the protective nature of an overworked Ego. This is, however, not what we want. Fear is too often an excessive modification of an impression or feeling that really shouldn't produce fear in us. We need to neutralize this tendency as much as we can. It is damaging to our projected reality to allow it to remain in place. To retrain it is not difficult and in no way does it damage us to modify it, as to do so gives way to a better life, a healthier ego and a happier existence. You cannot damage the intended and proper action of your ego. We have no ability to make the ego go away or stop working properly. We can merely bring the ego back into order and relieve it from the excessive strain we have placed upon it.

When the mind is overcrowded with thoughts and feelings created by fear, it takes on the character of an ***instinct***. In *Return to Zeropoint*, we are not studying to build up our state of mind. That might come later for us, but for now we must clean and clear out the chaotic confusion that feeds us error and prompts our ego to obstruct our path to enlightenment. It is much like stripping off the layers of an onion, one layer at a time, until there is no longer any extra chaff.

In the process of cleaning and clearing these chaotic confusions, we begin to discover our inspired enlightenment. Life transforms from one that has been solely led by conscious control to one of inspiration. Then we begin to soar like the eagles, unobstructed by the counterintuitive instincts that we developed from a manifestation of fear.

According to some philosophies such as Buddhism and Hinduism, the spiritual path is the process of meditating to move through our confusion and opening the hidden and awakened state of mind. If enlightenment were solely created by study, toil, and tremendous meditations, there could always be a return to the confused state of reality. Enlightenment resulting from the use of Ho'oponopono and *Return to Zeropoint* is lasting because we do not produce it; we merely become inspired by it and we always have access to it. In my estimation, the path to reaching the gift of enlightenment is far shorter with the use of this practice.

The absence of chaotic impressions and feelings within our Subconscious Mind relieves us from being crowded in with paranoia. It opens up a tremendous view of life, and that view begins to project a new and transmuted reality, a real problem-free existence. One discovers a completely different way of being. The I AM, or Divine Presence within us is well served. Yes, that is the Divine Consciousness within us; the I AM is always present and inseparable. I Am that I Am. The Kingdom of Heaven is within us.

Control Issues

We all desperately want to control — and specifically, we want to control all of our life experiences. Look at all of the things that we do to ensure that life turns out the way we want it to: we work jobs, we endeavor to work yet other types of jobs, we seek out mates, we negotiate so many things, we fight, we argue, we compromise, we get professional help, we exercise, we avoid exercise. What is the motivation for it all? It is merely conscious control issues, and they present a life filled with exhaustion and grief. We constantly seek to accept that we win some and then we lose some. Why would we fail to see that we are built to win all of the time? True, we might not always win as we hope to win, but we can win all the time. As long as our highest good is served well, we are winners.

We simply want our life experience to play out in a certain way: the way in which we envision it to be. We want to control the outcome of our lives. The desire to control life is so common to us all that we have given it a positive label: ***ambition***.

This ambition to control our own life outcome frequently spills over into our *Return to Zeropoint* practice. Repeatedly people use the practice of *Return to Zeropoint* with a specific mindset, a desired outcome, and a desire to direct. We tend to consider this as if it is ambition. It is not a good perspective for us to adopt in this practice.

Ask yourself these questions:

- Do I use *Return to Zeropoint* because I want my financial problems to end?
- Do I use *Return to Zeropoint* because I want to feel better?
- Do I use Ho'oponopono because I want to regain my physical health?
- Do I use Ho'oponopono because I want to control my life experience?

The answers should be simple: No. When you use *Return to Zeropoint*, you want to use it minus the preconceived outcomes. Do not use it because you want to feel better. Just use it to heal your mind, and if you truly work it as we teach you, you will remove all obstacles to success in love, health, and business in absolute peace and harmony. The perspective is what we stress here. Keep it clean, focus on healing, and let the outcome be your gift, not your expectation.

The serenity that we are usually able to find in a life without Ho'oponopono is dependent upon the level of expectation that we place on people, places, or experiences. It is human nature to expect Sally to act in a certain manner, and the manner in which she acts may either please or displease us. It seems natural for us to expect Fred to take out the garbage without being asked, because he usually does so. It is expected that our child's pediatrician would give our child the best possible care. What happens to us when our expectations are not met? We actually become engulfed in conflict, controversy and chaos when disappointment hits from unmet expectations. There is no place for that in the realm of Zeropoint. Those feelings are entirely counterproductive to our process. Use your mantra; clear and clean on these situations in order to make way for changes that will be acceptable and pleasing to you. Allow me to put it this way: We do not change anything. Things will change automatically. Trust in the process and it will serve you very well.

As the chaotic data begins to lift from within us, things also change on the outside. The right and proper outcome will occur. If you have a partner in life that excluded you from any financial decisions, totally disregarding your input and/or right to participate, it might cause you to feel offended and hurt. It could possibly foster some level of distrust. Look at those emotions, then clear and clean them. The situation will deflate, and either your partner will begin to include you, or you will decide to trust more, and it will not bother you any longer. Either way, it will only come from a healthier perspective and only your highest good is served by the outcome. Even though this may not be the outcome that you think that you desire, in all ways, and at all times, your highest good is always served, as you are turning the care and nurture of anything you clean on over to your higher self. Step away from the attachments to expecting specific outcomes. Allow proper outcome and nature to flow through the situation and become your solace. Trust in proper outcomes to find their way into your situation. If you look into this with your spiritual eyes, it will make perfect sense to you too.

As I write this, I live and work in a nation that is hard-pressed to stay financially solvent, just like so many individuals right now. Home foreclosures are widespread and retirement funds in large national companies have been hard hit with losses or wiped out altogether. Many jobs have left our country and gone abroad because corporations have sought less expensive overhead and salaries. The greedy corporations that sought lower wage employees in other nations also created many human rights abuses for the workers in those countries. There have been so many hardships inflicted along this path, and in too short a time for average folk to cope. People are actively clearing and cleaning on this, and jobs are beginning to come back home. What we really need is for many more people to begin engaging this cleaning. The people of the world hold this in their reality. We need larger numbers of focused clearing and cleaning, and the impact will be so positive, so beautiful, that many of the problems related to our economic difficulty will begin to clear up quickly.

This is not a political or economic discourse, but we all have had our share of concerns and fears regarding both personal and national financial security. No one has been immune to the disintegrating structure of global economic downturn. However, what is all this concern? It is merely dead, useless, and disruptive data running around inside my own subconscious mind. It is stuff that needs to be disposed of, and as I dispose of it, my reality changes. This stuff just creates chaos in our minds and that chaos just throws our reality for a ride, one that we probably will not enjoy.

Therefore, with this in mind, I am now cleaning my own thoughts of these circumstances. If this doubt and fear is allowed to continue within me, I shall never be able to recover my own former abundance and prosperity. I refuse to accept this so I clear and clean using the *Return to Zeropoint* system, and life and finances will improve in some fashion for me. I do not know how, nor do I dare to presume, but I have faith that they will.

One of the major facets of *Return to Zeropoint* is that, when it becomes a big part of our lives and we use it consistently, many things begin to change rapidly. In my own experience, work actually became more productive and financially rewarding. Income increased for me because of a new attitude and philosophy about my own abundance. I have enjoyed a return of my personal success once I began to develop *Return to Zeropoint*. I studied Ho'oponopono, began to use it, and an enhanced system evolved within me and it all helped me greatly. So much so, that I felt compelled to share it with you, and I remain committed to this great task. It is exhilarating for me to share this. I derive so much pleasure each time someone emails or calls, or gets my ear and tells me how their life is transforming for the better. It is a daily occurrence for me now, and I am feeling overwhelmingly blessed. Can I count upon you to use this and transform your life for the better, so that I can revel in the glory of the feeling that I may have done something to help you? I hope so.

My close friends that listened to me and tried it actually experienced the return of their former abundance too. I want the same for my readers and students. I am a firm believer that there is sufficient abundance for all of us to enjoy a better life. The only block between us and our share of abundance is our resistance to the gift of inspiration, and that gift is unlocked and becomes abundant as we clear and clean on everything.

I am a firm believer that this world is destined to change for the better, as those with insights and optimism have predicted repeatedly. The Mayan calendar has ended, the world did not come to ruin as Hollywood projected, and things are underway indicating a change for the better could be on the horizon. Be that change that the world needs. Imagine for a moment how huge the ripple effect could become as people begin to clear and clean on their life. Each person cleans on Mom and Dad, siblings, co-workers, friends, extended family, old boyfriends and girlfriends, and on and on. As you clean on each person in your own mind, your life becomes transformed by this action, as does theirs, and the world becomes sweeter and better for everyone. Just imagine how grand a massive movement could be to world peace and prosperity. It is just magical in concept. This is what I call a ripple effect of grand proportions.

However, before any big change fully takes place, there is often some upheaval. It is in a time of despair that non-believers will grab at anything new to try to bring about a change. The practice of *Return to Zeropoint* can ease the strain of any upheaval, and begin our shift from the former errant beliefs to the new way of thinking and being. In addition, we can reduce the discord.

Therefore, to put it succinctly, we have work to do. We should do it quickly to ease the pain involved to bring about the changes we must make in this time of strife. These changes will lead us into the better life that this new era promises for all of us.

A little bit about Religion and Philosophy

Return to Zeropoint and Ho'oponopono are not a religion or a replacement for any faith or religion. It does not violate any religious tenants. It is not heretical. In fact, it is in perfect alignment with all faiths and philosophies.

Kierkegaard, the great existentialist, did not believe that existentialism in any form conflicted with Christianity. He postulated that creating oneself seems to be not only possible but also necessary, if we take free will seriously—whether we choose for or against Divine Consciousness. For this reason, *Return to Zeropoint* represents no conflict for those who have no belief in a God.

Ho'oponopono can potentially empower people to change the relationship with self. Because of changing relationship with self, we come to discover a change in relationships with others.

Though *Return to Zeropoint* is not about manifestation of desires, it can change the way you draw good things to yourself. When we refer to change, we take it for granted that you understand that we mean positive change. It can change the circumstances of our own health, wealth, and well-being. We can affect those around us and across the globe, in the midst of a war, a life can and might be spared or saved. If enough people learn and use the practice of Ho'oponopono, the conditions of illness, poverty, and war could be stalled or eliminated. People are doing it as you read these words.

In my own home state, I hold regular meetings to work with a group on national and international issues of importance. We work on personal issues there too; if people care to share openly, we clean on them as a group. There is power in numbers when clearing and cleaning. Our objective is to create change, and changes come our way.

Others are teaching Ho'oponopono too. They actually do a fine job, but we believe that we have an expanded understanding and practice. This came to me from that increase in my own inspiration, then our use, and rigorous repeating of those techniques and practices in a variety of people. We had to prove to ourselves that this wasn't an accident or fluke. We had measurable change in rapid order and time. There was just no sense in denying it.

We all come from different backgrounds and different spiritual practices. We most likely come from different socio-economic groups and geographies. We come from different ethnic backgrounds too, and have up until now had different ambitions. None of that matters to us now. We have but similar amalgamated goals: world peace, national pride, health and success for us and for our loved ones. People really do have remarkably similar goals. We can all achieve them together, if we just apply the four beautiful and effective phrases that make up our mantra.

While approaches may vary, we personally felt compelled to offer an approach in which respect for each individual coming to us was paramount. Every person learns at the fastest pace that they are able. Only by being patient with those who might have questions can we help you reach the point where you recognize the ultimate unimportance of analyzing every aspect of this approach and simply becoming comfortable with its process.

We want to help you so that you may help us all to begin to change reality from within yourself, without pain, without stress, without pressure. There is so much out there for us to work on, and so little time to waste. We are empowered to build a better life, and a better world that is desirable, joyful, stress-free and healthy.

Ho'oponopono, the foundational beginning of *Return to Zeropoint* itself, is believed to have roots within an ancient tradition that predates nearly all of the world's existent spiritual paths. Many people believe that it arose from a tradition that actually predates the ancient Wisdom Schools, which were persecuted beginning in the fourth century. As a result, this inoffensive gift was necessarily hidden from view. It was taken away to the great detriment of society. Just think of how different the world could be today if it had all played out differently.

Realizing this, it also becomes understandable why these essential truths have found their way, closely held and guarded, into other cultures and traditions of wisdom schools. We at *Return to Zeropoint*, hope to share this wisdom and grace of our system with you for a better life and a hope filled tomorrow.

What is Reality?

This one key factor is very important to understand, as it is a core concept of *Return to Zeropoint*. We introduced this concept to you a little earlier on and would like to take some time to explain it to you and how it works. We know that it is a hard process for some to fully understand, but we want to make it more manageable for them.

As you stand in this world, at home, at work, at play, with family, with friends, with acquaintances, they all are a mere projection from within yourself. You are staring into a mirror, and you are 100% responsible for how all events you witness are played out. If you really resist this concept, I suggest you view the movie "*What the Bleep? Down the Rabbit Hole.*" It is unquestionably supported by many scientific discoveries that support our process.

We have need here to reiterate that our ego is an inflated tire that insulates the rim (life) from the lumps and bumps of the road we are traveling. At first, ego tends to get in the way of embracing the *Return to Zeropoint* and Ho'oponopono concepts. If you do not like someone who always does wrong in your eyes, why would you want to accept responsibility for their wrong action? We are the projector; everything we encounter is the screen. We really do stare into a mirror, and you will begin to understand this strange statement much better as you begin to practice the changes you will experience.

Examples: The angry salesperson that treats us with rude and inappropriate manners is highly irritating to us; the driver who acts out with road rage can scare us and cause us to feel threatened; the policeman or woman that gives us a hard time, making us squirm as they exert their apparent power upon us before giving us a ticket. All of these are examples of inappropriate uses of perceived power. Each opportunity is one upon which we can begin to clean immediately. Rapid response provides an opportunity for the circumstances to change in the midst of the problem. Don't wait for that ticket. Begin to clean on it the moment you are pulled over by a policeman or woman. Take the urgency out of the situation as soon as you can. It can create a world of difference for you.

If it happens to us, if we are subject to the difficult and wrongful circumstance, then we are compelled to realize that we have actually created it in the first place, all to get that dose of brain narcotics, endorphins. ***Total responsibility*** for all that we experience is what this is called, and it is essential to our understanding of Ho'oponopono and *Return to Zeropoint*. We must understand and accept the essential principle upon which our true and honest reality is actually founded. If we experience it, we created it. It does not matter that we may not understand what we did or how we did it, we simply created it.

You will soon begin to understand the relationship that these things depend upon. And no, your nasty relative is not at fault for you disliking him or her. You are responsible for their inappropriate behavior. In honest terms, blame never falls upon the other person; it belongs directed to faulty memory. This is what we focus our cleaning on - the way they cause us to feel. This is the greatest obstacle for ego to accept. It seems, on the surface, so much easier to place blame outside of our self. But it isn't though. It is much harder on us when we do that, and our poor ego suffers so much for it. We suffer so much for doing it.

Example: If you do not like your mother in law, it is because you created her into who and what she is by projection from within you. Again, you stare into a mirror. The things that we see that we do not like in others are manifestations of things that we need to create with that adrenalin, noradrenaline, cortisol and endorphin response again.

Creating Change Through Meditation

Meditation is an essential practice for us to master. Meditation opens channels for us and it should become a daily discipline. It is a constantly available communication tool for us. When I speak of meditation I mean the type of meditation that is a void where no word is spoken, and none is heard, except the slight soft whisper of Spirit. We just have to widen or broaden the path of communication and this will happen. This happens from developing a timely and consistent meditation practice. Having less chaotic data is a big help to broadening that pathway. Just focus on cleaning and clearing. The rest will fall into place by itself. Then begin a regular practice of putting yourself away from distraction and sound, and begin clearing your thoughts and enjoy of 30-minute visit to the land of emptiness, where everything is present to you.

Goals

The first and foremost goal in *Return to Zeropoint* is to realize that we want to be as clean and clear in subconscious thought as a child is. What is it that causes us to look at a baby as the most pure creature that we can have in our presence? Ever wonder why? I have, and now that I understand this system, I can see a clear answer to that question in my mind.

Babies are empty of confusing and conflicting thought (data.) They are PURE. They are naturally at Zeropoint. This is what we must strive to achieve with our practice of this tool. We must get back to Zeropoint, just like the child. We must erase bad data from our Subconscious Mind. To use positive affirmations can take up to 21 days; hypnosis can help if done correctly, and tapping as an Emotional Freedom Technique can too. But these are mostly conscious mind tools. The Ho'oponopono and *Return to Zeropoint* techniques are the fastest, most direct and can be self-administered.

Children are empty of chaotic and conflicting data, and they come and place no bad or erroneous data upon a situation. They are pure joy for us all. If you understand this point, you will begin to see why children actually have a natural spiritual nature, and why they so easily come from inspiration. They are empty enough to hear the inner message, and they slowly collect data, and slowly and progressively move outward from their innocence to the same chaotic state that we adults are usually in.

A man goes to work and is called into the office by his boss. The man is then chastised by his boss for something that he was not responsible for doing. As a result, he feels unjustly persecuted and his boss will not listen to reason. The man is hurt by the accusations and becomes angry and confused. He begins to change opinions of his boss and his job, and begins to dislike his position.

So, let's look at this problem. Where and how could he have mediated this problem?

1. His relationship with his boss was within his own experience, his own projection. He was completely responsible with creating the dead end situation. Maybe the situation would not be dead-ended, but it would be one that would have to be handled with intense effort. Since the boss did not want to listen to reason, he would have had a very hard time turning the situation around from conscious effort.

2. If he had paid attention to the manner in which it was causing him to feel, and used the 4 statements on each of those feelings, the situation would have most probably melted down into a more reasonable and manageable one because he would have ceased projecting errant or chaotic energy and thought into his field of experience.

3. With the help of Higher Self, via inspiration, had he known and used the *Return to Zeropoint* tools, correcting that error in his own experience and perception, his outcome might have been inspired. It very well could have led to great changes that might have catapult his standing with his boss instead of degrading the whole situation into a mess.

What he got instead was his adrenaline, noradrenaline, cortisol and endorphins. As I see it, he satisfied his craving for the cheese, but he lost important credibility at work with his boss, and he soured his own experience. That might be for just momentary, but he did not need or want the disturbance to affect him. He didn't need to create or reinforce negative neurons within his brain.

Please understand that this is not about some sort of guilt-trip. I am not saying that the man intentionally decided to create a bad relationship with his boss. All I am saying is that everything that we experience as the external world is actually nothing more than a reflection of something that is going on within our Subconscious Mind. Our experiences are always the perfect manifestation of our internal condition at any given moment.

I realize that if you had a long-term problem with your in-laws, and they are not accepting of you, that you will argue that they are guilty of acting wrongly toward you. I understand your point, but I am asking you to reserve judgment, try to be open to this, and reserve that judgment for a later time. As you try this on for size, as you begin to use the statements, you will begin to understand my arguments better.

We can all learn *Return to Zeropoint* techniques, to erase the errant and detrimental data in our Subconscious Mind. It is so unfortunate that this system of changing reality has been hidden from the broader society for so many years, a very long time indeed, and has only recently become known. There must be a reason, a grand plan in all this.

This is why it is not essential for someone to subscribe to any sort of belief in any kind of supernatural entity. *Return to Zeropoint* does not concern itself with such things, because it recognizes the essential unity of all phenomenon, and as such it understands that the Creator exists is within you. In addition, *Return to Zeropoint* rests solidly upon scientific principals, and affects memory receptors inside the brain in a positive manner. That science alone is enough proof to validate this methodology.

Recap

1. We are totally and completely responsible for all that we think, hear, read, face and experience.
2. I cannot fix anyone or anything but myself.

3. When we are in a tight or uncomfortable place and sense the need for change, we are to see how this situation makes us feel, and that is what we are to clean on with our statements.
4. We do not just clean on people, places or things that annoy, irritate or upset us.
5. We clean on our feelings and impressions of everything we encounter. Doing so prevents problems from coming into our reality.

CHAPTER 4
My Own Journey

I AM ENJOYING GREATER success in my daily life. This is true on a professional path, and in my relationships with friends, strangers and in my home life with my family. I am developing a psychic gift, which is happening naturally, and I sense the world around me in a different way. I appreciate the elements of earth, water, wind and fire from a broader perspective. I attribute these improvements to and in proportion to my use of *Return to Zeropoint*.

Now, if you want to begin with a prayer that entitles the higher self of Divine Consciousness and Super Conscious minds to help you in opening your awareness and aiding you in cleansing massive chaos and bad data, this might move things along a bit quicker for you. I just believe that every little bit helps. Try it; you have so little to lose, and everything to possibly gain from doing it.

Divine and Superconscious minds within me; If I, my family, relatives and ancestors have offended you in any manner or fashion, I ask your compassion and forgiveness. If I have offended or injured anyone, with whom I have had contact in any time or place, and have wronged in thoughts, words, deeds and actions; at any time or place, I ask your forgiveness. I love you; I am sorry, Please forgive me and thank you. Note: This is the prayer we say on Yom Kippur.

Let this cleanse, purify, release, cut all the negative memories, blocks, energies and confusion, and transmute these unwanted energies into pure light and love for all humanity, as I send my love to each and every instance, thought and memory and impulse within my collective mind. And so it is.

Intention vs. Inspiration

There is a distinct difference between intention and inspiration. Intention gets results some of the time, but it occasionally causes us trouble. Inspiration is from clear thought and higher self, but intention is from Conscious thought. In small matters, conscious thought can suffice. It is always used to decide when and what to eat; to decide what colored shirt to wear; whether to open the windows or use the air conditioner. In large and very serious matters, to use strictly conscious mind can be a bit more problematic. I use the analogy of the conscious mind as the cowboy, and the subconscious mind as the bull. The cowboy will mount the bull, but he will have a tremendous and upsetting ride. Sometimes he can stay on, but more often he will be thrown off. It's haphazard to try to control everything with conscious mind. We need inspiration. Inspiration is often flawless, and it keeps balance for us to use both the right and left hemispheres of the brain.

The Conscious Mind cannot compete with the capacity of Divine Consciousness, and inspiration is a gift to us from Divine Consciousness via our Superconscious Mind. The Divine knows no time, no obstacles, no constraints, so inspiration is a gift that knows a potential outcome. It is far-reaching and pure, honest and dependable.

Intention, as it comes from within Conscious and Subconscious Mind, knows only the illusion of our ***perceived reality***, the world we live in, or seem to live in. Intention is deciding to do something based upon my attitudes and opinions, using logic (the biggest illusion) to meet the demands of my perceived needs.

Despite coming from lower levels of mind, this may work out with satisfactory results, and then again, it may not.

If I were to decide to change jobs, ***without feeling inspiration***, but based solely upon my perceived needs and intent, I would probably only consider the most logical factors: salary requirements, work schedule, future possibilities for growth and synergy with superiors and/or co-workers. Those are conscious considerations. So if I decide to take that job based solely on those considerations, and a month or two later I am fired, I must ask myself if I was guilty of ignoring my inspiration. Inspiration uses not only creative thought, but can also include input from higher self, which often times has better sense than conscious mind. Inspiration versus intention - that is the difference between them, and the difference can be vast.

Inspiration might take me by surprise, and direct me to leave a job and move somewhere, or to initiate an offer, or some such business situation, and that might keep me safe and secure in the long run. We are not going to be misled. Higher Self has a way of knowing our needs, and it desires our needs to be met in a low stress manner with fewer problems. Intent, coming from my Conscious Mind, knows no such thing. It is akin to winging things.

In all manner and ways, and at all times, we still have our free will. It is not a crime if we choose not to act upon our inspiration, but before we discount it, we should clean with our Ho'oponopono skills to remove any doubt or concerns. Chances are that if we are in conflict about an inspiration, it is because we are not at Zeropoint. That means we are not clear enough at that moment to understand and interpret it. Not a concern, as we can clean and clear right at that moment. True inspiration will sustain and last through cleaning and clearing. False inspiration will not.

Again, if we make moves based solely upon our conscious intentions, before we initiate them, we should clean purposefully if there is any conflict or uncertainty about the outcome; stand steadfast to that safeguard, and don't make a move or a choice until you have done your inner work to clean. Cleaning can change the confusion into inspiration again, and help us to make a more clear and informed choice. It is a fail-safe manner of conducting our lives.

If I Heal Myself, I Heal My World

I worked on a problem with a friend of mine the other day. My friend had issues of guilt, because she wanted to travel from California to New York to visit her family and spend a holiday with them. By phone, her adult daughter imposed tremendous feelings of guilt at the idea of mommy leaving daddy alone for a holiday. Okay, I get that. In relating the story to me, she indicated that their funds were tight and both couldn't afford to travel, and hubby probably decided that he would cut himself some slack from pressure if he encouraged her travel to share in holiday joy with the family. After all, she works hard. He does not work; he cannot find a job, and he thinks he is too old for most companies to hire. He probably has some guilt from all these issues too.

This is where I went to work on her, but I did it as a lesson for her, with the intent of guiding and teaching her how to use the system to achieve a better outcome. I explained to her that she viewed money as something that was always passing her by. We cleaned on that thought. I told her that she had issues with her husband not working; we cleaned on that too. I told her that money is a tool that she felt unworthy of having; we cleaned on that as well. I told her that she did not believe that there was enough abundance for everyone in this world, and we cleaned on that. I also went out on a limb and told her that she viewed her husband as weak and ineffective. We REALLY cleaned on that. We did lots of cleaning that day.

Within 10 minutes, her cell phone rang, and it was her husband calling her. He informed her that airfares had just dropped two hundred dollars per person for the flight. They both could now afford to go on that mini vacation for that holiday.

She asked me if the change meant she should go. I had her do more cleaning on that question, and then I told her that she had free will and could go with him, go without him, or stay at home with him. All that changed was that they now had options that were added to the considerations. I told her that she has the free will and ability to exercise any of them, but we worked for a change in the situation, and a change came within minutes, just as I believed could happen.

They are going to be home together by choice, like a small family of two. Both are happy too, as they used their power of free will, with no constraints from financial pressure. Now, see it as created opportunity, or see it as chance that worked in her favor. The effect is the same, and I really am convinced it was in response to our work.

The World as You Experience It Is Not the Real Deal

Well, the title of this segment is true and untrue at the same time. The REAL world is perhaps made by the total intent of all the people within the many "individual worlds", so in fact my world is present to me, created entirely by me, and your world is present to you as created by you. If by chance you are an armchair physicist, do not throw this book in the fire or yell aloud that I must be out of my mind, because I even thought I was learning total fiction until I experienced this system for myself. Now I work and base my own words here on inspiration, not intent.

Here is a perspective: Science and religions alike teach us that time is an illusion. Science now has many theories about time and space that conflict with earlier beliefs. Many of these new theories now seem to lend credibility to our work. Many in science now consider our perception of space and time to be illusionary. So why should we be surprised to know that I have my immediate world, and you have yours? In my world, I have the power to co-create with the Divine, and you have the same power in your world. I am no different from you, not special, not gifted, and not magical. We all have this ability; there is no one that is less gifted. We are all equal in our relationship to the Divine, but some may just be more cooperative and getting better results than others do. This course gives us the tools and understanding to begin to get our own good results, our own satisfactions, triumphs, peace and health, and prosperity too.

To explain in yet another way, what is the REAL world all about? I wish I knew the answer to this. I have to do much more cleaning on that, and maybe I will begin to become inspired with the answer to that question. For now, I have enough to do to manage my own by controlling my own impulses, reducing my own intent, listening well to inspiration and creating that much deserved inner peace, health and harmony in my own world, my own existence. I do not have to worry about the outside space that I cannot control. I just know that the world as present to me, is a reflection of my inner chaos or inner peace: One or the other, or both at the same time. Can both co-exist? Sure they can, just think, start cleaning and get half way there, and then stop. Peace and harmony vs. chaotic thought, coexistent in one space at one time.

You Do Not Have to Know How or Why Data Got There!

How did this happen to me? We all tend to ask that, as if we knew the answer, perhaps we would be able to stop it from happening to us. Do not worry about it. Let it go. If you feel that an answer is necessary, then clean on it until that quagmire disappears. It's chaotic data that confuses us. Your Subconscious Mind can be compared to a hard drive on a computer. It is a storage device. We can't control everything with our Conscious Mind, but through our Conscious Mind, we do allow error to get in somehow-

some way, and likewise, in error, or whatever, we are living the life that the Subconscious Mind has created for us in response to the chaos of that data just running around in an infinite manner in our Subconscious Mind. It just has to be cleaned out and light from the Divine will fill the new void. We don't require knowledge of how it got there to clean it. All we have to do is allow inspiration to help us in our job of how to clean it up and get rid of it. It will help you just as it helps me. All parts will begin to work together in harmony for the right outcome.

Exploring the Solutions

To SOLVE problems you need to answer: Who am I? And who is in charge?

Who am I?

I am the temple where Divine Consciousness resides. I AM that I AM. To reiterate the words attributed to Jesus: "The kingdom of heaven is within you" and " Believe me when I say that I am in the Father and the Father is in me; or at least believe on the evidence of the miracles themselves." Now, if you have read these or heard these phrases before, did you think that they were only meant for Jesus? He taught these words along with many other clues, because they pertain to all of us. We are the ones that are supposed to take them to heart and learn from them, but again, the laws and illusions of time and space lie to us, as we have been told by science and religions, and we have accepted them and their limited concepts as gospel truth. All illusionary, all deceptive, except for those who learn these truths. We are the temples of the Divine Consciousness, the I AM. Together, through constant association and love, we co-create our reality. I am a co-creator with the Divine whom rests within me. Together we are one. I am empowered, through love and free will, to co-create a world of joy or a world of pain. I have the power within myself to make any world I choose to make. That is who I am. I create a reality all of my own. **I AM that I AM.**

Who is in charge?

I am in charge, always and under all circumstances. We have FREE WILL. Never look outside for control. It is always within. Again, we assume 100% personal responsibility for all things present to us and within our experience; they are ALL of our creation. If you want things to change, clean inside you, and by so doing, create the opportunity for those wanted changes. The intellect is only conscious of 15-20 bits of information per second out of millions of bits stored in subconscious thoughts. Do not try to search your mind for answers.

Here is where you get another sense of how powerful the Subconscious Mind is compared to the Conscious Mind. One clearly has tens of thousands more "thoughts" or "data" than the other. The Subconscious Mind churns an infinite number of thoughts per minute. Your Conscious Mind is no match for its ability or agility, but it does get chaotic and confuses or changes outcomes that are less than desirable.

Just think about how your mind works when you meet a new boss or someone like an attorney that is about to rapid fire question you. You churn thoughts and impressions at a staggering pace. Little bits of seemingly related thought enter into your Conscious Mind as you begin to assess whether they are friend or foe, fair or devious, true or false, etc. You read changes in expression, body language, speech patterns, and choice of delivery in speech patterns as you rapidly analyze the person. It is all part of your assessment skills and most of it is buried in your Subconscious Mind.

Now, in your ability to assess a person, have you ever thought back and wondered how you could have gotten it so wrong; been so far off base? Considering that this element of your mind has creative ability, paints your world for you, and still has the ability to erroneously judge in assessment skills, then why would we be surprised at it painting an erroneous outer world for us? It is not so far reaching at all. We know that we make mistakes all the time. It's common; we're human. In effect, that Subconscious Mind pushes data forward to the Conscious Mind at its own pace, at its own discretion, at its whim. This is how our world takes form and shape. This is how we get it right sometimes, and wrong other times.

The whole idea of cleaning and clearing with our *Return to Zeropoint* skills begins to offer new hope and a promise for a more orderly and desirable experience in life.

IF NOT the Intellect, WHO or WHAT is in charge?

This is where we get the religious spill over. When people get disappointments in life, like family illness, and pray incessantly, and then say "when we don't get what we're asking for, we get something even better, because God knows what we really need," that's defeatist thinking. The Divine is a gift-giver for sure, but surely not a selfish one, a sneaky one, or a stingy one. We make a constant error, we tend to pray outside, as if to heaven exists in the sky. Realize your inherent power. You are a co-creator.

Memories Dictate the Experience

We experience something early in life, and it makes an impression. Maybe we witnessed a serious argument or fight between family members. That etches peptides deep into our memory, and it is not in the forefront of our mind, or in the Conscious Mind, unless we call it there by trying to remember it. It resides hidden within the subconscious, and occasionally we recall the incidents, or perhaps we forget all about it. Either way, it's still there, tucked into place, and the subconscious compares against it constantly.

A new relationship begins years later in our lives; perhaps the person has the same hair color or similar appearance as the family member did in our story, the perceived antagonist. At times, this may present with similar characteristics in the person(s) that might resemble our antagonistic family member(s) who created or participated in the family argument. Maybe they are not fighting, but maybe always edging toward provoking one. This is from drawing upon a distant memory and projecting it into another person at a later time, without logic, understanding or minus our conscious thought.

Clean on people as you meet them, and this will not happen to you. In the case of a person you are just meeting, you have no predestined negative experience with them, so your cleaning is simple; with them in mind, you have only to say to yourself; I love you; I thank you; I bless you. That's all there is to it.

Before you walk into a room you should clean it this way. Going to work, clean on the workspace before entering into it, and before going to church, to the doctor, clean before you walk in. Everywhere you go, clean before you enter. If you meet objectionable people, clean specifics with your four statements, according to your impressions and feelings, but always, always clean

The World Resides in the Subconscious Mind

Quite often, we imagine that this aggregate of senses and experiences, which we identify as the "body" or "me" exists somewhere in time and space as a "reality," but this is not the case. What we perceive as everything and ourselves in our world exists only in the Mind, and is the direct result of the data, playing largely as memories, that can be found therein.

As Shakespeare wrote, "The world is a stage..." and that stage exists within your Subconscious Mind. Our objective through the practice of *Return to Zeropoint* is to help you move from this sense of being ruled by memories (data) to a place where you free your mind to receive inspiration, thus transforming your experience of the world and all that is perceived as being "in it".

The Superconscious Mind does NOT generate ideas, feelings or actions

The Superconscious Mind, what we commonly call "soul," does not originate thought. It is an interpreter, taking inspiration from the Divine and as it deciphers it, transmits it to Subconscious and Conscious Mind.

For the sake of an example, let us say that Divine wants to inspire you to move to Fiji. The inspiration is sent to the Superconscious as a package. The Superconscious, a gentle and meek area of mind, unpacks it, translates it, and shares it as an active thought by sharing it with your Conscious Mind. You receive the message and you are inspired. We usually take credit for the genius thought. Most often, we fail to recognize that it is Divinely inspired and take all the credit for the sheer genius, and then feel all plumped up over it. I still try to do this as autonomic response to my own inspirations. Once I begin cleaning on them, I then get the better picture as the inspiration coming from Divine isn't chaotic or negative. It remains, through the cleaning, becoming clearer in its origin and intent. Then we are free to choose whether or not to act upon it. When you decide to act upon inspiration—once clear that it is inspiration, not error— clean to test it, and only if it remains and continues to inspire you, then act.

The Subconscious Mind does NOT generate experiences

It is essential to realize that the Subconscious Mind does NOT generate experiences of its OWN, BUT it experiences memories, it FEELS as memories FEEL, it BEHAVES as memories BEHAVE, and it DECIDES as memories DECIDE.

The Subconscious Mind generates stored memories and impressions, taken from previous experiences, sometimes with things that never had anything to do with the fact that the previous situations might have really been different. It's like having mental pollution when chaos is the result. This is where problems are generated and projected from within us, onto others or places, or experiences that we create. If your sibling is fighting with you and expressing anger, it could have come from an impression you had when you were a child, or maybe some stranger and less important memory than that, as a story you read, or a movie you watched. It's okay, as we are allowed to enjoy movie and television entertainment. Entertainment is a good thing, and relaxes us and brings us needed rest and diversion.

Clean before and after you watch a movie or read a book. That way you protect your Subconscious Mind from absorbing wrong information from the storyline. A story should be just that - a story. Cleaning makes the difference. It is crucial in problem solving to realize that the body and the world are not the problems in and of themselves, but merely the consequences of memories playing in the subconscious. Right now, this may seem abstract to you, but as you begin to use this system, you will begin to understand this point much better, or accept it more fully.

Are My Family and Friends Real?

Of course, they are real. They are as real as anything else is real. They are as we project them to be, but yes, they are real; they are just our personal version of our own reality. Here is a breakdown of how we project family, friends, acquaintances, co-workers, etc....

In our "universe" of creation, we have family, friends, associates, and acquaintances who come our way. We observe and may even note intrinsic behaviors within these people, and we are not necessarily the only ones that observe these behaviors. This does not mean that they are not of our creation. The more people that observe what we observe in our friends shows that they are all, collectively, just a mirror of our internal mental projections. In this manner, there is synchronicity, agreement and similar observations of the one. This is not just true of the one person, but is the same for all of them. Hard to grasp at first, but those other people are merely a projection of our Subconscious Mind as well. It is normal and natural that they will see exactly what we see in that one person. Their ratification of our observations that one person does not prove that what we observe is truly outside of ourselves, it just proves how well we can project and create. Every once in a while, you might encounter someone who disagrees with your projection, and in their experience, the subject of our projection actually behaves very different in the other person's reality.

When you look around a room full of people, and note their differences, you can begin to get a sense of how powerful we really are as co-creators. We do far better than any Hollywood scriptwriter at making a tremendously vast world all around us.

My friend's mom fell down last week, and within one day she could barely move it at all, despite the x-rays showing no sign of broken bones. Soft tissue injuries are very real and can be quite painful. They sometimes take as long as a fracture to heal. Read the excerpt from his email to me:

> "I began cleaning and clearing to relieve why I may have caused her situation. While doing so, I treated her painful areas with a *Return to Zeropoint* Wand. I did the wand treatment on her while cleaning because I did not believe the problem was in her shoulder, where she thought it was, but rather felt inspired that it was a twisted muscle in her arm.
>
> Her arm rapidly became warm, and as I just sat there, sipping my tea and cleaning (myself), she began to get very sleepy, almost like she had taken pain medication. When she came over to see me the next

day, she was amazed that she had no residual pain, and again had almost a full range of motion. I kept cleaning and one day later she is at 100% range of motion. All that improvement happened in just in two days. What a tremendous difference. Awesome result in record time!"

There's no word for the level of gratitude I feel each and every time I get results like this. I never tire of it, never get bored of it and actually get the giggles each time I see that I can control my reality, and improve the lives of myself and others with my *Return to Zeropoint* techniques.

The First Few Times

During the beginning of your journey to *Return to Zeropoint*, your Ego will usually try to interfere and attempt to shield you from accepting any degree of personal responsibility. This is normal to feel and it should be expected. As I stated earlier, our Ego has had to grow to enormous proportions in order to shield us from our lifetime full of difficulties, as we have had a skewed perception of what constitutes our true reality. I recommend using the previously mentioned set-up statement each time you are going to use the system, to gently train and exercise your own deeper understanding. Do this for a while, maybe a whole week, until it is no longer presents a problem for you.

What we have come to refer to as one's "soul" – that is to say the Subconscious and Conscious Mind collectively, does not generate ideas, feelings or actions on its own. It is simply a "playback device" for the data – the memories – that serve as the basis of those interpretations (feelings, actions, ideas).

The soul "sees" what the memory data has recorded; it "feels" based on memory/data; and it "behaves" informed by memory/data.

None of these have any basis in reality. They are all perceptions and often flawed.

It is crucial in problem solving to recognize that the body and the world are not the problems in and of themselves, but the consequences of memories PLAYING in the subconscious. Remember the mouse in the lab; it's all about recreating situations that will provide that endorphin dosing to our brain.

A Closer Look at Zeropoint

Zeropoint is the cleaning and clearing of memories that continually project problems into our reality. The cleaning and clearing relieve the projections that continually bring us problems and situations that create difficulty and stress.

The Universe began with Zero and will RETURN to Zero. Zeropoint energy in outer space exists within the void as explained earlier. That void, referred to as "dark matter" has a trillion times more energy than the dense matter of stars, asteroids and planets do. Imagine that. Pure energy, highly charged energy, and every planetary shift from moment to moment cause high impact.

In us, the Zeropoint of void created by cleaning, natural to a baby, is what I believe to be much the same as the void of outer space. This is where the real energy is, the wondrous and powerful energy. The energy of intelligence and inspiration is within that void.

Memories or fractured and chaotic data that are replaying on the "hard drive" of your Subconscious Mind overshadow and project the awareness of your True Nature (Zeropoint). When cluttered, we find ourselves identifying with external phenomena, and imagine that this body or this situation, illness, or condition is collectively "who" we are. We forget that we are empty of all inherent qualities – the VOID or Zeropoint Energy in its purest form. We are the very essence of the ultimate energy that this universe is built upon.

By cleaning and erasing these renegade memories, we transform the data back into Zeropoint, much like erasing a hard drive restores it to its empty and "unformatted" state.

Common Ground, the EQUALISER of your True Identity

This Zeropoint state is the indestructible and timeless foundation of the entire cosmos. It is becoming recognized by scientists, but many years ago was recognized by those such as Albert Einstein, as being "empty" or a void. Buddha Sakyamuni referred to it as the ultimate reality – stating that all phenomena are inherently empty, some 2,500-3,000 years before Einstein's discovery. Because it is emptiness, the Zeropoint Field cannot be destroyed. Memories only obscure and displace our awareness of it and our reliance upon it. The Conscious Mind has the power to initiate the *Return to Zeropoint* process to release chaotic memories or data rather than engaging them with blame, self loathing, low self esteem and many other common thoughts.

The Ancients Understood This

While our first and primary focus in this book has been, at least in part, the ancient practice of Ho'oponopono, the awareness and recognition of the more complete teachings of the *Return to Zeropoint* methods, and the essential process of clearing our data and attachments goes back very far into the past. There are similar but less effective methods found in Dharma faiths and philosophies like Buddhism, Taoism, and the Bön tradition of ancient history. I personally know of many people who follow the Dharma traditions and prefer the use of *Return to Zeropoint* to aid their practices, because it is direct, speedy, and gets them to the desired state of Zeropoint much quicker than the deep meditative states that don't clean as fast or as well as Ho'oponopono.

In the ancient Bön (Bön predates the Buddhism) and Tibetan monasteries, monks recognized that various crystals and minerals resonated at the same frequencies as the four "clearing phrases" of *I love you*; *I am sorry*; *please forgive me*; and *thank you*. They also understood that whenever items that vibrated at these frequencies came in contact with the body or with other natural substances, such as water, air, or vegetation, they changed the vibrational frequencies of those items as quickly, helping to restore them to their own "Zeropoint" or true potential nature. All life forms recognize this force and flourish in that presence. I believe that this is founded upon sacred geometry and is the same or similar to the vibrations emitted by the Golden Rule of mathematics known as the Fibonacci Sequence.

Thus, when someone was experiencing pain, or inflammation, bringing the combination of specific crystals to the area that was manifesting inflammation, would aid the body's water content to remember its balanced origins (homeostasis) and it would clear away the very inflammation that was manifesting as a disease state.

From this ancient research, which was most likely given to them by the Awakened Ones themselves, who resided in the Ancient Far East, they developed healing tools or clearing devices, which included the precursor to our Zeropoint Wand. I only wish science could and would jump in here, to help us all fully understand the wonders of this effect, but they have shown no interest thus far.

Once the *Return to Zeropoint* Process Begins, It Continues

Return to Zeropoint is an action using logic and proper order to transmute memories back into VOID. When we initiate the process, we are saying:

> "I acknowledge that my problems are of my own origin. They are nothing more than dualistic garbage data replaying in my Subconscious Mind, and for this, I take 100% responsibility."

This petition process moves downward from the Conscious Mind into the Subconscious Mind, which relies on instruction from the Conscious Mind, much like a child relies on instruction from his mother.

Maintaining the Zeropoint state requires frequent cleaning. Memories and associated errant data are constant companions of the Subconscious Mind. Memories never cease their incessant replaying. They never leave the Subconscious Mind to go on holiday.

To completely dispose of memories for once and for all, they must be cleaned and returned to nothingness, transmuted for once and for all. Once done, you need to move forward doing more of the same cleaning, because they tend to add up quickly.

Remember, your true nature is indestructible and eternal emptiness—Divine Intelligence, without form or beginning. The physical form of the world we witness is the expression of projections taking place within the data of the Subconscious Mind.

By eliminating the erroneous thoughts and memories playing at the subconscious level, the state of the physical world changes to reflect the effect of "cleaning".

CHAPTER 5:
The Advanced Techniques

WHILE IT IS POSSIBLE for you to completely transform your life by relying on the four powerful *Return to Zeropoint* phrases, the analogy between our minds and our modern day computers affords opportunities to do some "advanced" healing work, for even faster results.

These are the strategies and techniques we teach during our advanced intensive, but for the purpose of helping you to understand what they, we will list them here:

- Recognizing the multiple facets of every experience. It's all data... but arises from different places.
- Understanding the Body-Mind connection in Health.
- Spiritual Mind Treatments replace defective data, helps facilitate returning to Zero.
- Meditation—the practice of resting in Pure Awareness.
- How to send a blessing forward to change the "mood."

Return to Zeropoint is a petition to Divine Intelligence that is made to transmute chaotic or errant memories to void. Work it and work it well. It is cause for miracles to appear in your life.

"Seek and you shall find, knock and the door shall be opened for you"

What you ask for in this regard, as it is the plan of Divine Consciousness, shall be granted. As you begin the *Return to Zeropoint* practice, work the system for what it's worth. The door opens to Divine Consciousness, and it is that consciousness that reaches down into your Subconscious Mind and cleans it out as you request it.

What you ask for in this regard is granted according to the will of the Divine. That was how it came to be; the system was given. It is a direct petition, to use the power of co-creation to its max, to achieve the unachievable, so to speak. You have the power; use it. This is the program that Divine Consciousness wanted to use, to increase our capabilities for creating good--not bad, for health, not disease, for peace, not war.

We, individually, have no control over what to keep and what to discard in our Subconscious Mind. It is a vast and huge recorder. It does not have the ability to discriminate what it will store and what it will discard. We have to work to empty this hard drive as much as possible. We don't need to keep corrupt chaotic data there. Clean it out; get rid of it. All it will do is make life more difficult and stressful. Remember my question earlier: "did you ever notice that whenever there is a problem, you are always there?" That's the corrupt and chaotic data causing that. We have to clean, clean, clean.

Let's look a little more at this whole idea of asking, seeking, knocking...

There is an account in the Christian scripture, which tells of Rabbi Jesus teaching His disciples "the Secret"... not the one popularized by DVD and YouTube video... the original Secret:

Ask. Seek. Knock.

There is nothing mundane here. The power lies in the promises that follow the instruction: *"Ask, and it shall be given to you. Seek, and you shall find. Knock, that doors may be opened to you."* And it was a point He felt was important enough to reiterate the teaching, *"For everyone who asks receives, and who seeks finds, and to the one who knocks, it shall be opened."*

ASK...

Have you ever asked your mom for cookies as a child, only to be told, "No, not now, they will spoil your dinner"? I'm sure that this has happened. And perhaps the next time we asked, we would try to do so a little earlier in the day, or maybe even after dinner. Eventually, we found the right time to ask for those cookies.

We learn by continuing to ask, and gradually learning our parents' mind, and learning what is ultimately best for us. The author of the book attributed to the Apostle John wrote: *"This is the confidence we have in approaching God: that if we ask anything according to Divine Will, God hears us. And if we know that God hears us — whatever we ask — we know that we have what we asked of It."* (1 John 5:14-15)

So our petitions, when in proper spiritual alignment (Right Intention) — in other words, when what we ask for will edify, build and bless ourselves and others around us — then we receive or manifest what we need.

SEEK...

The secret is to seek the Will that exists within our higher self... (See a theme recurring here?) And we will find abundance poured out for us. For those of us who don't embrace a belief in gods and such, the Divine Will is another expression for the Greater Good, which is another powerful promise all on its own.

KNOCK...

Have you ever knocked on an open door? I'm certain it is not a regular habit for you. Knocking is something we usually do when the door is closed. Doors opening can be a metaphor for opportunities opening to us. If we knock on the doors that appear closed, having sought the Greater Good, and asked for those things we want, opportunities will open to us.

A point often overlooked in the English translations of the Scriptures is that when Jesus' words were recorded in this account, Matthew uses the imperative present tense. Therefore, a more accurate translation from the Greek and Aramaic would say:

"*Keep on asking, and it will be given to you; Keep on seeking, and you will find; keep on Knocking, and it will be opened to you. For everyone who keeps asking receives, and who keeps seeking finds, and to the one who always knocks, it shall be opened.*"

"Therefore whatever you desire for others to do to you, you shall also do to them; for this is the law and the prophets." (Matthew 7:12)

Let us resolve to keep asking, continue seeking, and always knock when doors seem closed. And *Return to Zeropoint* can help you do just that.

The SOUL can be INSPIRED by Divine Intelligence WITHOUT knowing what is going on

So, as explained earlier, we redefine soul as Super consciousness. It is the interpreter between Divine Consciousness and lower forms of thought, Conscious and Subconscious Minds. What we receive from Divine Consciousness cannot be directly interpreted or utilized without passing through Super consciousness. It reaches into both Subconscious and Conscious Minds. It knows when and how to facilitate the cleaning as offered from Divine Consciousness, and how to interpret and transfer inspiration from Divine Consciousness into both subconscious thought and conscious thought so that we can act upon it.

If you begin in disbelief, as I did, not to worry. It still works. That's the problem I have with other concepts that promise miracles. If you do not believe in the miracle, the miracle will not happen for you. Well, if something is true and real, it should work well for you as long as you operate it correctly. Belief is not necessary to get this system of cleaning and clearing to work for you. Go through the steps and use it. It will prove itself out for you, just as it did for me.

Reality and *Return to Zeropoint*. Will I die?

What is real? Is life, as we came to believe in it truly the real thing? Of course it is. Your reality is in front of you as you project it, but life is real just the same, and along our path, we must come to realize that part of our reality is that we are merely of human form. As human, we have a beginning and an end, but that is to the human form alone. We are also ***pure spirit***, and as such, we have ***no*** end. We remain intact and whole after our life here, without the human form attachment. Human experience is one phase of our real life, and this IS a reality.

The religions of the world have taught us this concept for time eternal. Life is endless. Mediums communicate with those that have left this world of the living, without difficulty. That is something that I consider a spiritual gift. Churches denounce that, as they realize that they cannot control it. I understand that well enough. However, it does not change the fact that some of us have had extraordinary experiences by seeking the counsel of good psychics.

Why would we experience this and then doubt that life is eternal? Well, the answer is rather simple. We tend to disbelieve anything that we can't validate by touching, smelling, hearing, seeing, tasting. We rely upon our five senses to affirm what we suspect. None of our five senses has the ability to reach beyond this world and experience them. I take it on faith. I have had extraordinary messages brought to me from beyond. I have had experiences that would defy explanation by rationale, but were outstanding, true, and real. I have seen enough, and I believe anyway. That is how it is with *Return to Zeropoint* and me. I have seen enough, and I believe with all of my heart.

Just because we are proponents of a system of altering our reality doesn't mean we give up on the world and the best it has to offer us. Maybe there are lessons to be learned or even taught along a path that includes chemotherapy or treatment for a disease such as cancer. One thing for sure, we DO NOT ever throw out the baby with the bath water. Common sense is important and prudent, just do not allow deception to cloud you. Always employ cleaning, and it will invariably lead you to a right choice, and this includes fighting against a disease.

Return to Zeropoint is a petition to Divine Intelligence is made to transmute memories to void for creating good, not bad; for health, not disease; for peace, not war. We, individually, have no control over what to keep and what to discard in our Subconscious Mind. It is a vast and huge recorder. We do not have the ability to discriminate what it will store and what it will discard. We have to work to empty the chaotic data from this hard drive as much as possible. We do not need to keep connections to corrupt data in place there. Clean it out; get rid of it. All it will do is make life more difficult and stressful if we hold onto it. Remember my question earlier: "did you ever notice that whenever there is a problem, you are always there?" That is the corrupt and chaotic data causing replaying of old tapes in our memory. We have to clean, clean, clean.

Being in conflict with another person strains our relationships with everyone. I've recently had to confront some very serious issues in which my trust had been violated, and someone close continued to make decisions that were deeply disappointing and caused considerable emotional stress and heartbreak for a number of people closest to them. And while I initially experienced anger over having just spoken with them about this precise matter a few months earlier, I found the hours that followed to be a cycle of anger, frustration, hurt and imbalance. It is pervasive in its nature.

I knew that forgiveness would be a process, and would not pretend that the negative consequences of this person's actions were just going to magically go away. In fact, I am very clear that this person needs to fix what they did, even if it means their being inconvenienced, or having to sacrifice their own leisure-time plans until they can do so.

But I am also clear that remaining in that cycle of anger, hurt and frustration will do nothing to resolve the conflict. I have allowed myself to feel the wound and have avoided the easier path of denying that it hurt me. I have spent time realizing that damage was indeed done to the relationship, and the loss of trust has had a profound impact. And those things are in fact, the first steps toward healing.

You see, when we deny the pain, our focus internally is on the pain. We don't want others, especially the person or persons involved, to know we were vulnerable. And so that interior focus creates adamant need for retribution... we want to restore the balance to the relationship, and the ego imagines that hurting someone back will do that. But it never does.

Forgiveness means being in favor of (for-) the process of giving. Giving compassion. Giving understanding. Giving room for the other person to make right the things they said or did.

More importantly, anger and resentment are products of incorrectly placing the "blame" on someone other than us. When we function from Pure Consciousness, we assume 100% responsibility for our experiences, and there can be no need or room for blame.

Each of us has the capacity for bringing the sacred into every situation. The pain and wounded nature of any circumstance is soothed the moment we generate true compassion for the "other" person, and recognize that every experience is an external reflection of something within us that needed to be healed.

The person who hurt us is also hurting. There is no time or need for regrets over times when we violated someone's trust in us, or when someone else violates our trust. When we forgive ourselves, we naturally forgive all others. When we learn that the sole purpose of this physical experience and body, created by the ego-mind, is so that we can learn those lessons needed for our spiritual progress, then we can let go of the need to label things as "good" or "bad".

That does not mean ignoring the emotions that arise, because those emotions are also our teachers. Nevertheless, it means allowing ourselves to move through the pain... through the crisis... and to do what we must, in order to ensure that we do not find ourselves in that situation again. Sometimes what we have to do is difficult. Sometimes it means coming to grips with the reality that someone else might not care about the damage they have done to us, because they are incapable of anything more than self-absorbed, immature and self-destructive behaviors. But other times it may be an opportunity for the other person to reach out to us and lean on us to help them get those self-destructive, immature and self-absorbed behaviors under control, so that they can leave them in the past.

If we are stuck in the mode of anger and retribution, we will always miss the opportunity to be there for others.

Moreover, when we are angry with one person, it influences every relationship we have on the planet. You cannot be angry or out-of-accord with one person, and not have disturbed the balance of your relationships with others. This is because your very nature is love, not discord, and when you are not acting out of love, then you are not in accord with your true nature. Therefore, you have handed-over the control to the ego, and are not functioning naturally.

For this reason, we can mindfully turn to the Four Phrases, and allow ourselves to experience the forgiveness, which must begin with ourselves, as we say: "*I love you. I am sorry. Please forgive me. Thank you.*" The moment we do that, we are speaking words of immense power into our core, and they resonate throughout the Universe. On a quantum level, the vibrational quality of the experience is instantly transformed. The heaviness, intensity and drama begins to dissolve, and we suddenly realize we have the power to heal that situation.

Again, this isn't some hocus-pocus or new age parlor trick—it's about assuming 100% responsibility for our experiences, and recognizing that we have the capacity to transmute pain, anger, resentment and suffering.

Choose forgiveness. Choose peace. Choose love.

Forgiveness is not something we do about the past. It's something we do about the present moment.

Being Proactive... Supplementing the *Return to Zeropoint* Process

Practically speaking, there is no need to do anything else but clean, using the *Return to Zeropoint* techniques; however, the reality is that we are conditioned to be thinkers. Moreover, it can seem daunting at first to clear the data, when right behind it; we are creating new data, only to have to clear that data, etc.

In the section below, excerpted from one of our *Return to Zeropoint* intensives we shared some observations on one way to further support the clearing process, by using spiritual mind treatment and questions to replace the defective data.

Non-Judgment and Intentionality

There was an article, in 2010, in Tricycle magazine, in which Matthieu Ricard, gave a wonderful interview on science, meditation and happiness. In it, Ricard, who was a scientist before entering a Buddhist monastery, states quite lucidly, "Thus Buddhist science is not just an intellectual pursuit for the sake of unravelling the mystery of nature, but it also has a therapeutic aspect that gets to the very basic cause of suffering. In this context, a rigorous pursuit of science is not to hold a blind belief in anything but to honestly and eagerly pursue the investigation of the mechanism of happiness and suffering."

Life responds to intentionality and thought. Intentions are used to guide our attention and creative energy in a specific direction, in order to accomplish or realize a certain goal or objective.

The most important thing to consider when looking at your intentions is to let go of the tendency to judge things as "good" or "bad". For example, if you are dissatisfied with your current job, you may think it is time to focus on finding a "better job". Already you have set yourself up for suffering, because you're getting caught up in a dualistic approach to life. Look at your present situation as simply being what it is. And understand you are the only person responsible for everything that goes on in your experiences. You may not be able to control what others do, or how events unfold, but you are ultimately in control of how you respond to those things.

Think back to when you first started your present job. Remember how it seemed like the "perfect fit" at the beginning? Allow yourself to recognize that everything is impermanent, and that includes our jobs and careers. When something has served its purpose, it naturally and organically needs to gently be let go.

Know that the flow of life is always moving forward, and that the perfect situation already exists for you. State your intentions aloud, "My next job is satisfying and rewarding. It flows with me, brings good to the world, and allows me to grow and prosper." Then quiet yourself and allow yourself to see yourself in the perfect job for this moment. What does it look like? What does it feel like? Notice what you are doing in that particular visualization... what is your job? Now know that what seems "perfect" in this moment is usually just a reflection of our self-cherishing tendency to grasp at whatever things we imagine will make us happy. If we are ever going to realize perfect happiness, we have to stop looking for external sources, because they will always ultimately cause suffering.

See your job for what it is... a relationship... an opportunity to mutually agree upon terms by which you exchange one thing (compensation) for something else (time/skill/effort for money). And that money is simply something you use as a new medium of exchange... etc. The only real purpose of your job is to provide for yourself and for your loved ones.

No more need for anxiety, tension, or fear. Allow life to unfold with you simply along as an impartial observer. Take time each day, even if only for ten minutes, to practice sitting silently, and allow your thoughts to come and go without judging them. It can be the most liberating 15 minutes of your life!

When we begin to realize that every thought is just data... just some bits of information assembled mostly as a result of past experiences, memories, fears and perceptions... it's easy to begin to allow our reaction to those thoughts to become more neutral.

Return to Zeropoint allows us to "erase" the data on the "hard drive" of our Subconscious Mind, something that will ultimately free us by allowing us to "return" to Zeropoint (we're not actually returning anywhere, because we are always at Zeropoint. What's happening is that we are returning our awareness to the recognition of this truth, and allowing ourselves to release the data that obscures that awareness from our lives permanently).

However, if you had a computer with corrupt information on it (like the data playing on your subconscious level), and you knew that over time, a simple repair could be done to eliminate that data and wipe your hard drive clean, you would have two choices: and for your hard drive to be restored to a blank (Zeropoint) state, or—data, which creates the kinds of experiences you want to have, which is what happens when we engage the science of "spiritual mind treatment" in conjunction with our *Return to Zeropoint* practice.

Let's look at an example. Let's say that you're working on cleaning the data, which manifests as financial difficulties in your life. While you engage the *Return to Zeropoint* practice, and begin cleaning the memories from your Subconscious Mind, you could consciously replace that data with what we call "spiritual mind treatment".

Below is an example of a spiritual mind treatment that one great teacher, Rev. Ernie Chu wrote, which focuses on allowing Divine Consciousness to support us in every aspect of our lives.

Rev. Chu's spiritual mind treatment happens to be framed in a much more theistic context than some readers might generally find relevant or useful, but the underlying message is, nonetheless, applicable — that you and I are Love/Energy/Zeropoint expressing Itself, and that we, as creators of our experience, have the limitless potential to create a new and better world.

Whenever I engage in spiritual mind treatment, I like to employ the strategy of asking questions as a means of furthering the manifestation process, so that when a particular affirmation or treatment comes from a context that might be foreign or less "familiar" to our own preferred context, we have the opportunity to re-frame the affirmations in our questions.

To help illustrate how that works, I thought I would share with you an example of a proposed journal entry, so that you can see how I would use this process personally. First, we'll begin with Rev. Chu's Spiritual Mind Treatment:

> I Let Divine Presence Support Me
>
> I celebrate and acknowledge the presence of the Creator within me; the I AM, which is all loving and present in every part of my life.
>
> I know this to be my Source of All Good, because Divine Consciousness fills my life with so many gifts. I am whole because I am loved and I AM.

I know that it is through the gift of love, manifesting as creativity in my life, that I joyfully express myself as a wondrous aspect of God, through the opportunities that I create, and the enterprises which come into form through my relationship with the Infinite Presence.

I create a prosperous, creative and joyous life, expressing as ventures, companies, ideas to be developed, and other businesses, fully knowing that I create these as part of my wholeness with Spirit and my personal expression of Divine Consciousness in action.

I give great thanks; knowing gratitude also as Love.

And release this to become a part of my experience, and God's support and Love.

And so it is.

Now, let me share how I used this particular treatment with you. It felt religious to me, but that is Rev. Chu's thrust, and I was tempted to discard it and go to another example. But that's when I decided to use this as an opportunity to share how we can turn around such things to become part of a more inclusive, expressive and useful process of manifestation and demonstration in our lives.

Take a look:

Why do I let "divine presence" support me?

Divine Presence? I know that what we imagine to be a "divine presence" in our lives is, in reality, Emptiness... that pervasive and all encompassing, creative reservoir of energy from which all things manifests. I choose to use Love as a more suitable metaphor and frame of reference in my life. I let Love support me, because it is "the eternal principle". For this reason, I celebrate Love, and recognize it as my Source of all Supply.

Why do I express myself through the opportunities I create, and the enterprises, which come into form, as a Perfect Manifestation of Love? If love is the eternal principle, and indeed the only "reality" then I choose to see beyond the dualistic ideas and perceptions, and know that at any given moment, I am exactly where I need to be, expressing and manifesting this Love in my life.

Why do I create these opportunities and experiences?

I create these because it is my nature commands that I express Love, for the ultimate purpose of a great inner awakening, and so that I can help to alleviate suffering in all the sentient beings that I can.

This was a wonderful experience, in which we had the opportunity to learn how the mind works in its creative process. You see, simply repeating a Spiritual Mind Treatment that might contain words or ideas that we disagree with or cannot relate to will never yield the kinds of results we need or desire. Thinking otherwise is simply illogical.

You see, our Subconscious Mind never responds to ordinary statements. That is the domain of the Conscious Mind. The Subconscious Mind responds only to queries. This is why we take this two-fold approach, speaking to our Conscious and Subconscious Minds simultaneously, so that the subconscious can begin creating the answers to the questions, and the Conscious Mind can begin acting upon the realization of our True Nature. Inspiration vs. Intent: I'll choose inspiration, as it brings gifts.

This is what Arthur C. Clarke meant, when he commented, "I don't pretend to have all the answers. But the questions are sure worth thinking about." That is the realm of genius. When you ask yourself a question, your mind automatically begins looking for an answer... and that unlocks the creative impulse within you. Creative Impulse, my dear reader, is truly the gift of Inspiration.

"Rather than making a statement you may not believe, why not ask yourself a question that can transform your life?" - Dr. Noah St. John, productivity expert and author of "The Secret Code of Success"

Let me explain my own belief about this emptiness

Throughout this teaching, I make constant reference to being empty, that place of Zeropoint that we strive to attain, as the place of emptiness. Well, it is true, but only in part. Science has in recent times developed a new construct for the substance of what we refer to as "dark matter." It is believed by many to be the glue of the universe, the very unknown glue that directs and guides the movement of planets. It is strong, even though its nature is perhaps unknown, but they realize it is there, and it is massive in its capacity to direct all universal life.

I imagine that the substance of Zeropoint is quite the same. It is a high-energy form of space that we can not see, touch, feel, or properly identify. However, it is there and it is awesome in its presence and ability to infuse us with constant goodness. I hope this helps us to realize that Zeropoint, the desirable place to be, is a place of extreme benefit.

The thing that is different in *Return to Zeropoint*, is merely the method that I use to teach Ho'oponopono. Many teachers give a little bit of information. I try to give you the honest, complete and useful method to help you achieve that state of Zeropoint. As such, I have a tool that I often use when I am beginning a workshop or seminar. This tool is designed to relax our ego, condition the subconscious to receive our statements, and make the flow into a stream of goodness that is less challenging for us to trust. If I do not use it, I find that ego throws its block into the mix, and confusion reigns supreme. That is how we have conditioned and trained our ego. When this happens, nothing makes sense to the audience. Data would begin playing, and people would become so objectionable to the process. I've seen it happen with other teachers, and they are labouring and challenged to bridge this condition, and I find it to be nonsense. This tool is heaven sent.

I shall share this with you, and it will also be inside our *Return to Zeropoint* workbook, so that we cut through this data like a hot knife cuts through butter. It saves me time, and in our workshop, I have much to teach about this system, and I want to be assured that people get it right and walk away with a viable system of understanding so that they can begin to change their lives.

Great Superconscious Mind, I will now begin to use phrases to cleanse our Subconscious Mind and set it into an orderly and clean state, to relieve the chaotic data that is so damaging to our well being. I do this for the benefit of projecting a better reality for myself and for all others in my life. I will begin to heal myself of disease, and I ask you to pay attention and heed my instructions, as they will create a joyful existence and experience for us in this life.

Ego, I ask you to stand aside, and allow us room to heal and repair from error in thought, in word and in deed. This is essential for us to accomplish in this life, as I must learn these lessons well.

Divine Consciousness, I ask you to guide us in the needed tasks, and make manifest the knowledge that will benefit this life experience, for the good of all humanity and for this beautiful earth that we call home. I ask you to increase within me, and help me to mature in wisdom, to complete this task for wholeness and goodness.

To all error and ego standing in the way of success in this task of learning what I must learn to accomplish wholeness:
I love you
I am sorry
Please forgive me
Thank you

To all parts of my mind and body, and to all of nature:
I love you
I thank you
I bless you

And so it is.

Chapter 6:
The Importance of Your Blessing

The Hawaiian culture vastly differs from the Mainland culture. I think it is safe to assume that since this great tool came to us from Hawaii, they may know a little more about the truth of reality than we do. I think that as we use Ho'oponopono faithfully, we too will begin to know. We will come to know a great many truths.

One of the truths that the indigenous Polynesian people of Hawaii know is that everything created by the hand of man, woman, or child is actually created by a person endowed with the gift as a co-creator. As such, everything that is created has an actual life of its own. Wherever there is life, there is also memory. Before you get your morning coffee cup into your hand, clean on it. Do that same thing until every dish, cup, glass and piece of silverware in your home is cleared and cleaned. From that point forward, clean on new things brought into the house for the first time. Keep your home and all its furnishings clean and clear. This is your home, your sanctuary, and your castle. Help it to be energetically peaceful and happy.

Every single aspect of creation, including items created by others, has memory attached to it. Yes, the car, the coffee cup, and the commode you sit on. If one of them came from a factory where the owner had financial problems, you can absorb that negative energy. There can be many reasons for failure in life, but the least decent reason should be the coffee cup you hold onto, or the commode you sit on or the car you drive in. Get with the program, and you will begin to understand these statements well. You will change your entire world of existence.

We Constantly Get in the Way of Life.

We plan so hard. We stress so well. We figure, plan, and stress all over the place, and we rarely allow life to unfold for us. It is understandable, coming from normal thought process. We are so comfortable with utter control, leaving nothing to chance. It's understandable to me how we do that. I spent my whole life doing just that. Most people do. It is amazing to me now, and I cannot really understand that under those circumstances, how we actually manage to get anything at all accomplished.

Do you accept that we contain the Divine Consciousness within us? If God really exists within us, and we are in the role of co-creators, then we have the power to bless. I do not mean that we issue a blessing in the same manner as a church might issue a blessing; I mean a **real** blessing, one that works.

What is the most important attribute of life? LOVE is the most important attribute of life. I'm sure that you probably agree. Well that is where I begin with issuing a blessing—I state my love:

1. **I love you**

   Once we establish that we love, we might be inclined to issue the blessing itself. So our second statement in this three part system of blessing is:

2. **I bless you**

   Then, when we have stated that we love something or someone, and we bless them, we have felt and used our inner power in a construct that builds goodness and grace. We should begin to realize that as we do this, we are the big winners, as our reward comes to us simultaneously. Yes, we grow from it, we expand from blessing the elements and our homes and our cars, etc.

   Therefore, as we realize that we gain from issuing a blessing, and gifts are something we need to appreciate, our third and final statement is to say thanks.

3. **I thank you**
   Done, final, we have issued a blessing with three statements, and it is merely a manner of sending our love into a situation. All things and people behave better, when love is shared so as to comfort them. It is highly energizing.

Memories

Everything has memory. Not just people. We have a visible head that we know contains a brain, but memory comes in other forms too, not just in brain matter. Muscles have memory too, and certain plastics have memory Did you know that one of the biggest memory capacity elements on our planet is contained within water? I know that as true because when I discovered this fact, I was amazed, excited, and it put me into a state of awe. I see water in an entirely different light than I ever did before.

I began this journey with water by watching a YouTube video. It was a famous Japanese doctor (Imoto) that put three carafes on a shelf about 1 foot apart from one another. Dr. Imoto opened a bag of ordinary rice grains, and placed an equal amount in each of the 3 carafes. From one pitcher of water, he poured an equal amount of the water into each of the 3 carafes, to a level slightly above the rice. He then covered each carafe and his experiment began. For 30 consecutive days he approached each carafe and issued the following statements.

Carafe number 1: I thank you

Carafe number 2: I hate you

Carafe number 3: he said nothing

This was an experiment designed to show that energy is transferred from the words we speak to objects such as water and rice. In the experiences of most people, water and rice are inanimate objects that serve a purpose. Again, the statements were repeated to each carafe individually for 30 days. At the end of the 30 days, each carafe was filmed to display the result. The results were nothing short of amazing.

The 1st carafe, the thank you carafe, had developed a fermentation process that released a sweet smelling, golden color ferment.

The 2nd carafe that had hate projected at it turned rotten and black and reflected the foul smell that we might expect.

The 3rd carafe, the one with nothing stated to it, had streaks that reflected light golden color and streaks of black rot.

This visual example is an invaluable example of how our words have power. Words are things. In this instance, they prove our intent has power: the power that only a co-creator can demonstrate.

Dr. Imoto performed many experiments with water that are available on YouTube and in his books. He has displayed in a very adept manner for all of science to witness, that water responds to our emotions and our words. Water is a living thing, with memory and a job to do for us, and it does it for us with love and respect. All this from two molecules of hydrogen bound to one molecule of oxygen. Both are gasses at normal atmospheric pressures, yet when combined, they become liquid. Water is one of the few things that I know of that can exist in three states: liquid, steam and frozen. Through all three states, it never forgets what it is. Amazing.

Many experiments with water have illustrated that words such as our 3 phrase blessings: *I love you; I bless you; I thank you*, have the ability to change the structure of water. Once stated, then frozen, sliced paper thin, then examined under a microscope, the results exhibit the most beautiful crystalline structure that one could imagine. Conversely, negative words, and negative sounds have demonstrated a change that reflects what we would assume negativity to reflect: chaos.

Science challenged Dr. Imoto and his findings. At this point in time, scientists all over the world have replicated and demonstrated that Dr. Imoto knew what he was talking about and he knows his science. That is not too farfetched to believe, since we see all forms of science and its theories begin to crumble. Science has been learning that we have operated upon a set of false theories for a long time.

During the period of World War II, a group of high-level scientists assembled into a conference room in the city of Tokyo. Japan's was attempting to construct a pathogen or poison that was suitable for biological warfare. As each scientist was there to demonstrate and defend his own belief that his method would produce a more desirable result, they had hours of argument and battle in trying to sell their concept as the one that would be used. The conference room that they occupied permeated with their anger. They were shouting, arguing and a definite desire to inflict deep damage onto an opponent in war was the rule of the day in that meeting.

Worthy to note: there was nothing else in the room except a table and some chairs, the scientists with their notepads and documents, and a pitcher of water with some glasses was on the table.

The meeting of the malevolent scientists abruptly ended midday. Everyone in that room became severely ill, some actually passed out. They had exhibited signs of extreme poisoning. They were transported to a hospital. Emergency care was administered in a manner consistent with the symptoms of poisoning. Their blood was drawn, and not one of them had any viral, bacterial or chemical poison within their bodies that could make them sick.

Now in retrospect, there is a prevalent theory that it was their anger, their vitriol that actually changed the energetic composition of the water in that pitcher. The water transformed and took upon itself the energy of the biological warfare that they argued to use against their enemy. That water was taken from the room, as sabotage was suspect, and was handed to a laboratory for rigorous scientific examination. It was only water. Nothing else had been added to it that would make it poisonous, yet the scientists in that room almost died from consuming it. Yes, there was real illness in them, but no visible reason, no poison, bacteria or virus was evident in their bodies.

Words are things. Everything in our world that is food, and everything created by hand of humanity has a memory. Allow this to sink in. Just think for a moment about how loving water is. It exists to support us: its mission is to do for us all the things that we normally expect it to do. On that day in Tokyo, water for drinking was present, but as their focus was poisoning, and their intent was strong, their argument was forceful, the result and impact from the water they drank was deadly. The water behaved according to the *intention* of the people within that room. The water was never malevolent; it behaved exactly as they argued and wanted biological warfare to behave.

So as I began to understand this, just as you might be beginning to understand it now, I now step each day into my shower and continually repeat my 3 phrases to the water that I shower under. It just so happens that we do absorb water when we shower. The difference in me that 1st day was noticeable to others. I heard comments from people that actually saw a noticeable difference in me that was obvious.

There are other methods and resources for clearing water and increasing its energy. You can write the three phrases on paper, and place it under or tape it onto a carafe and allow a few minutes for it to energize it. Proven fact; it works. In addition, you can use the Zeropoint Wand to energize water or any liquid. It not only energizes the water you are going to drink, it also influences the nature of the water in your body by compacting the molecules, and has the unique ability to ease the pain in a joint or of an injury. As the water in our very tissues is influenced and energized, it takes away the inflammation.

Then there is the Fibonacci sequence, and its energetic effect upon water. In 1202, Leonardo of Pisa, a mathematician dubbed "Fibonacci" created what has been named as the "Fibonacci Sequence." The sequence is known as the "Golden Rule" of mathematics. Many of the early Gregorian Chants were written with an embedded Fibonacci Sequence of musical notes within them, as they were believed to impart superior understanding and wisdom to those that heard them.

A very special carafe has been designed that has the sequence exhibited in rungs on the carafe itself, and when water is put into the carafe, it is charged and ready to consume in 3.5 minutes. The effect: in drinking, it feels like a heavier texture as you swallow it. Put this transformed water into cut flowers and watch them take a new life and vibrancy upon themselves. Put it in plants and it will outperform any fertilizer or plant food. Amazing things happen. The wand accomplishes this too. I always make the lettuce for my salad fresher by using water energized by my wand or from my Carafe. I always soak any veggies in that treated water before cooking, and my living plants are thriving.

Now, in my shower, I keep plastic encased Rare Earth magnets on the pipe that comes out of the wall to my showerhead. This similarly changes the water and energizes it too. Add to that the three statements: WOW.

Lightning clears waters memory and returns it to its natural state. The natural state of water that is cleared and cleaned actually counterbalances pollution. I am of the opinion that lightning also does similarly to the soil.

High voltage discharge, such as ionizers that erase the negative memory of treated city water that has travelled through pipes that make many 90 degree turns and been infused with ammonia, chlorine and fluorides. Chemicals and treatments have a negative affect on water, removing its natural properties. This can be restored by any of these methods.

Back to business:

If you were planning a big dinner and friends were invited, and you were going to teach them something important to you, that you believed they would benefit from, would you plan it down to the last detail? Or would you trust inspiration enough to let go of utter control, allowing it to unfold into life-stream?

We do get in the way, always, all the time, until we learn to trust that inner voice that provides suitable inspiration that will ensure all goes well. To state it another way: We wander aimlessly through life, trying to find our way and means. Our resistance ensures that we remain anxious, and then we realize spiritual starvation, mental confusion, physical illness and financial distress.

I know that this takes a great deal for granted. That is one of the reasons I suggest you read this book twice. Maybe read it three or four times. Gain your training wheels, learn to use the system, grow in faith that it works, and then begin to trust in the inspiration that begins to flow freely within you. It has been said that for each bit of conscious data, one million bits goes on in subconscious thought. Those one million bits of thought contribute nothing for our success in life and love.

I cannot begin to tell you why this took all this time to become known. Maybe it is not important. Maybe we would not have considered it very important if we were not living the very challenges that today's world provides for us. However, at the very least, it is here right now. This time is the moment and it is the opportunity. We would be hard pressed to ignore it, considering it takes so little effort and promises so much goodness in return.

Ho'oponopono, the foundational basis for the *Return to Zeropoint* system, came from a very old culture. Even if we take it as just Hawaiian, on that alone, it is very old. Many old cultures, including the Polynesian culture, teach that everything created that is in existence has a life and memory of its own. According to their beliefs, if you walk into a banquet room where you plan to hold a function, it may actually be feeling old and tired from wear and tear, and as such, it can contribute to a down note to the event you are planning.

Sound crazy? Just try to remove every obstacle to your event. Clean it, and offer it your love. The experience of loving it will be such an "up" note for the hall, that it will cast a different and more uplifting mood to your event. Here is an example of how to do just that.

Sit in the room on any day before your event. Feel the room; allow inspiration to move in you. If you are at Zeropoint, you might hear the answer. Ask the room permission to hold an event there. Motivate it. Give it love by saying, "I love you" in *Return to Zeropoint* fashion; send that forward to appease and motivate goodness to come forth from the very room you will host your event in. Do not worry that you might not actually feel real love for a room. Just say it repeatedly, until you begin to feel it. Trust that the room will provide a better environment after giving it your love than it would have without that love.

If a building or place is created, built, and a place where many people have been, it can actually be tired and fed up. I would be; and so would you. Ask permission from the room, offer the love, and consider it something so little to give up from within, that it really costs you nothing but a moment of thought and concern. You have so much to gain. Allow inspiration to carry you. The very old culture that carried this method for so many years would not think of doing without such a small step to insure a better and happier result. I know this may sound crazy to you because it is not a common behavior in our culture, but just give it a try and do it. It takes so little time and effort, and the results can be tremendous.

In this teaching so far, we have challenged so many of your previous notions of how and why things work for us, that one more isn't going to cost anything. Break the habit of disbelief with working this system of changing life and all it circumstances. Leave nothing to waste. Include it all, clean it all, make your world as healthy and problem free as you can. Remember the rule, you are the projector; the world is your screen. Direct a good movie with your intent to build a better life for yourself. Clean everything. Appreciate everything under creation; love it all.

I have long held this belief. Our happiness is not dependent upon the love others give to us. It is dependent, solely; upon how much love we give out. Many very well loved people have committed suicide. Receiving love from family and friends did not do it for them. They were sick, and they actually felt dead inside before they took action to terminate their lives. Do not be one of them.

Burn these words into your memory. They are true and they prove out. It does not just apply to people or a banquet room. It applies to the beautiful sky, the clouds, the blooms on the bush, the cars, your home, the building where you work, the tools you use, and all that you touch, use and determine to be to your potential advantage.

Love it all. Watch how your life becomes one of extreme joy. Send your love to it all before you walk into the door and enter the space. I dare you to try and then tell me it failed. It will not fail, as it cannot fail. It never fails.

I know that many might tend to paint me as a dreamer by reading these words. I am now, but I was not a very good dreamer before. I am learning though. I want you to learn too, to love all the things in your path. Love your way into a beautiful life and path.

I walk into work the same way each day as I have many days before *Return to Zeropoint* became reality. Before, people might utter a hello to me as I passed by. Now they come to me and they want a hug. My love goes right back to them. I am a happy man. They feel it, they see it, and they want it too. Oh, how I want to share this joy and happiness with you too. I want it for you desperately. I am filled with joy, and want you to experience that. Imagine how our world will change with all that inner peace.

The eternal message is love. Love as we are loved. Give love freely, and watch it bounce back to us tenfold. It is such a pleasurable experience, such a thrill to live this type of life. There is so much to appreciate in life. Loving it all is just the next step.

When you clean, you will begin to see everyone just as the Divine Consciousness sees him or her. As you see with those eyes, you will quickly learn what it is all about. The Kingdom of Heaven is within you!

Personal Loss

Everyone will experience loss of friends, family and partners. The finality of loss is a moment when we come to think that there is no further chance for change. This could not be further from the truth. Every relationship has a beginning and an end to it. Your relationship with your physical being has a beginning and an end and this is the proper ebb and flow of life. We would not want to go on forever with the same patterns and situations. We come forth, develop, mature, command and form, and then retreat to source. The same is true with a relationship of family and friends. They have the same ebb and flow, so death is hard for us to get through, but we always do get through it. Life does really go on, despite how convinced we were that it wouldn't. It is supposed to go on, and it will always go on. Thank heaven for that fact, as there is always something to learn, room to grow and something for us to conquer.

But then those relationships that break up, like the married couple that were together for 40+ years and he goes out to find a young replacement. Wow, this is a tough one on a conscious level; but on a subconscious level, it is from within self, and is merely a projection of our own fear of aging and we project this trauma into our experience because it provides a huge chance for a big dose of endorphins. It is so excessive a situation for a little bit of endorphins that only last a few moments. It just is not worth that little bit of drug. I choose the path of joy, of wisdom, of light and of love. So, I don't wait for it to come to me, I choose to create it for myself. I want more than anything else in my life to impress upon you that it is the easier path to take. Be bold, do it for yourself and all the people you love. Clean and clear your path to super happiness.

Relationships

We all have relationships. I have a relationship with the person I have lived with for many years. I have a relationship with my boss, my co-workers, my clients, and my students. I have relationships with my family, friends, and all the casual people I meet along the path of life. This includes the people I meet at the grocer, the bank, the dry cleaner and the shoe repair shop.

These examples are only partial in scope. I illustrated them to help you understand and to jog your mind in possible opportunities to clear and clean. As I finished this last line of text, I froze up with writers block. Imagine that! Oh, it has happened a few times while writing this book, so I just step away from the computer and I clean and clear on my creative state regarding the process of writing. I took a phone call from a friend, and while we discussed her problem with a relationship, it came to me. Like magic, inspiration came back to me, and with this inspired word, I will finish my teaching for this book.

Take out a notebook. On the top of each page, write the name of a person in your life, someone presently there, or someone past. Under that name, write attributes of your relationship with that person that bothers you. Take a moment, under that attribute, write how each one causes you to feel about your relationship to them. Clean and clear on those feelings you wish were different. Some things might take a few repeats of the mantra, and occasionally you might spend a considerable amount of time on it, but you will eventually get to your goal. We have incidents in school as children that we should clean on, and the memory of the spanking we got when we were young, but as you treat them and all the family, all the friends, and all the co-workers and incidental folk you know in life, you will be clean and clear, and at Zeropoint. The good thing about this, is that they will too. You serve yourself a real great gift to clean yourself, and as a gift to you, they clear too. That's the ripple effect we make in our world.

To remain there, keep that methodology in mind, and the next time you go to a store where a salesperson is unresponsive to your needs, or belligerent, clean and clear right there and then, and you will remain at Zeropoint.

I wish you well in your use of Ho'oponopono, and remember, when you walk into any building, get in any car, bus, plane or train, send your blessing to it. Clean it, clear it and tell it you love it, thank it and bless it. This will remove so much grief.

I hope we will cross paths some day soon. I hope to meet everyone. This is the reward I ask for: to hear your stories of success, your abundant joy in life, and to feel your love, as you already have mine.

> I wish abundant blessings upon you.
> I love you
> I thank you
> I bless you.
>
> And for the success of this teaching and all
> the rewards for you and for me:
> I love you
> I am sorry
> Please forgive me
> Thank you
>
> Affectionately, with warm regards and
> appreciation for you, my reader,
>
> Robert Ray

Resources:

Return to Zeropoint **website:** *www.returntozeropoint.com*

Made in the USA
Middletown, DE
31 October 2017